INDEPENDENT ED

INDEPENDENT ED

INSIDE A CAREER OF BIG DREAMS,
LITTLE MOVIES, AND THE
TWELVE BEST DAYS OF MY LIFE

EDWARD BURNS

WITH TODD GOLD

AVERY
an imprint of Penguin Random House / New York

AVERY

an imprint of Penguin Random House LLC
375 Hudson Street
New York, New York 10014

Most Avery books are available at special quantity discounts for bulk purchase for sales promotions,
premiums, fund-raising, and educational needs. Special books or book excerpts also can be created to fit
specific needs. For details, write SpecialMarkets@penguinrandomhouse.com.

The Library of Congress has catalogued the hardcover edition as follows:

Burns, Edward, date.
Inside a career of big dreams, little movies, and the twelve best days of my life / Edward Burns ;
with Todd Gold.
p.   cm.
ISBN 978-1-592-40859-7
1. Burns, Edward, date.   2. Actors—United States—Biography.   3. Screenwriters—United States—
Biography.   4. Motion picture producers and directors—United States—Biography.
I. Gold, Todd.   II. Title.
PN2287.B865A3   2015   2014029408
791.4302'33092—dc23
[B]

ISBN 978-1-59240-933-4 (paperback)

Printed in the United States of America
1   3   5   7   9   10   8   6   4   2

Book design by Elke Sigal

To the Kids

CONTENTS

CONTENTS

INTRODUCTION

My first film was released in 1995. It was *The Brothers McMullen*, a comedy about family, relationships, sibling rivalry, and growing up after you're already grown up. Shot for $25,000 in and around my parents' Long Island home, it won the Grand Jury Prize at Sundance, scored at the box office, and got me labeled as one of Hollywood's hottest young independent filmmakers. A few years later, I couldn't get a movie made.

You should know that I did not set out to become an indie filmmaker or to make an independent film. I've never given any consideration to those labels and definitions. Besides, what is an indie film? Some people argue that it has to do with subject matter. Some people think it has to do with the size of your budget. Others believe it has to do with how you got your financing or who distributed your film. I've always defined it as a film that is independent of outside influence. And that's all I wanted. The goal has been to make films—my own films—on my terms, the way I have envisioned them, without any interference. And that last part is tough to pull off. It has required belief, courage, and an unflinching streak of independence. The result has been a labor filled with far more love than frustration, and far more a sense of accomplishment than defeat. And that's the story I have told in this book.

As of January 2015, it will have been twenty years since I took *McMullen* to Sundance. Since then, I have written and directed another ten films. Many of them have had seven-figure budgets (my biggest budget was *No Looking Back*'s $5.5 million); my last three have cost so little they have been labeled microbudgets. To dwell on the budgets, though, would be to focus on the wrong thing. *Independent Ed* is about my education as a filmmaker, a producer, and a writer. It's the kind of book I would have wanted to read back when I was in film school or before then, back when I first got the idea of writing scripts and putting those stories on film. In those days, I didn't even know if making a movie was possible. More important, I didn't know it was impossible. I was dumb enough and young enough to believe in my dreams. I like to think I still am. Dumb enough, that is.

Which is the message I hope to convey here. In this book, you will read about how I have made movies, why I have made them, and what happened along the way. You will see that the business side of making films is as crucial as the creative process. But nothing can replace the commitment you have to make to your work. If you want to make a film, you simply have to find a way to make it. An important thing to remember: There are no rules when chasing your filmmaking dreams.

That's the big takeaway. There is no right way or wrong way to make a movie. You've just got to figure out a way to get it done. And it won't be easy. But that's not why we do it, is it? We do it because we have no choice. It's who we are. And most likely, you'll find that those days on set will be the best days of your life.

Eddie Burns
Tribeca, New York City
2014

INDEPENDENT ED

The middle of three children, I was raised in a neighborhood of Irish, Italian, and Jewish families in Valley Stream, Long Island. My dad, Edward J. Burns, was a sergeant with the NYPD. Later, he became the department's media spokesman. My mom, Molly, worked for the FAA and has to get the credit for turning me on to Woody Allen.

Soon after we got our first VCR, sometime in the early eighties, she brought home a VHS copy of *Take the Money and Run*, which, needless to say, I loved. That was soon followed by *Bananas* and *Sleeper*. A few years later, it was *Annie Hall* and *Manhattan*.

But at this point, I had never given any thought to how movies got made or who wrote them, and I certainly had no dreams of becoming a writer myself. Not yet. But my father did.

When I was in sixth grade, I wrote a poem that won first prize in the Catholic Daughters of the Americas Long Island poetry contest. It impressed my dad, and from then on he always encouraged me to write and tried to turn me on to writers and novels he thought I might enjoy. One day he came home with two books, a collection of Eugene O'Neill plays and J. D. Salinger's *Catcher in the Rye*. I never looked at the O'Neill plays, but I immediately fell in love with Salinger's classic coming-of-age story. It was after taking the journey with Holden Caulfield that I first thought about the possibilities of telling stories of my own.

I was always a pretty good storyteller. You had to be in my house if you wanted to get airtime at the dinner table. I also never had any problem sitting down for a few hours to tackle a creative writing assignment at school. That was not true of my science fair projects, and I usually received good grades and encouragement from my English teachers over the years. My senior year of high school, I wrote a short story that my English teacher, Mrs. Maxwell, thought was terrific. But much to my dismay, she wanted to include it in the school's literary magazine. I was at first absolutely against this. I thought the story was too sensitive, and I knew my friends would rag on me endlessly. I did not need that abuse going into my last summer before college. However, after sleeping on it, I said okay—but with one condition. I asked her not to put my name on it. I would get the satisfaction of seeing my work in print and I wouldn't have to worry about my reputation.

Thankfully, Mrs. Maxwell ignored my request. She published the story with my byline, and while there was a fair bit of ball-breaking from my friends, some were impressed, and the girls . . . well, long story short, when I went away to college, I thought maybe I would become a writer. I was a pretty good student and a pretty good athlete. If I wasn't playing ball, I was watching it on TV or reading about it in the sports pages. So I figured maybe I'd be a sportswriter.

I started my college career at SUNY Oneonta in Upstate New York while being wait-listed at SUNY Albany. After one semester at Oneonta, I was accepted to Albany, where I soon declared myself an English major. During my sophomore year, I started to entertain the idea of becoming a novelist. The picture I had in my head of a novelist's life appealed to my nineteen-year-old's sensibilities. I'd write during the day and go out at night. I was getting good feedback on a handful of short stories I had written and decided it was time to start my first novel. I got about fifteen pages into it and realized I was not going to be a novelist. The major issue being that I was enjoying too many nights out and not enough time in front of the typewriter and in the classroom.

I was put on academic probation, and it turned out to be a blessing. My advisor issued a blunt warning but also offered a stay-in-school-and-don't-get-your-ass-kicked-by-your-father strategy.

"Look, if you don't get your grades up, you're going to get kicked out of school," he said. "But as an English major, you can become a Film Studies minor, where you watch a bunch of old movies, write a paper, and you're pretty much guaranteed an A. You'll get a couple of A's, get your GPA up, and we won't have to kick you out of school. What do you say?"

The next semester, I took my first film appreciation class. It was called Four Directors, and it focused on Orson Welles, John Ford, Alfred Hitchcock, and Billy Wilder. I was enamored from day one. These men were the heart of the lineup of post–World War II filmmakers, and I tried to watch every film they made.

On the first day, we watched Wilder's Academy Award–winning

classic *The Apartment,* which I immediately flipped for because it reminded me of the Woody Allen films I loved. It was a New York comedy, small and intimate, and it felt honest. After seeing it, I went up to the professor and asked, "All right, who is this guy Wilder? Tell me everything. Fill me in."

A Jew from Austria, Wilder fled Hitler and Nazi Germany, where he had worked as a journalist in Paris and then Hollywood. In 1939, he cowrote *Ninotchka,* which earned his first Academy Award nomination and heralded the arrival of an unparalleled talent.

The real pleasure of learning about Wilder, though, was watching *Double Indemnity, The Lost Weekend, Sunset Boulevard, The Seven Year Itch,* and *Some Like It Hot.* His range was astounding, and he wrote *and* directed like Woody Allen—my reference point in any discussion of film at the time. Now I had another master to revere.

I spent that semester devouring film. I was constantly searching for new discoveries. I watched everything: Hollywood classics, French New Wave, Film Noir, Westerns, Italian Neorealism, and of course the great American films of the late sixties and early seventies.

One such film from that era was the Peter Bogdanovich coming-of-age movie *The Last Picture Show* starring Cybill Shepherd and Timothy Bottoms as high schoolers in West Texas, and watching it was a life-changing experience, as good art is. You're one person before, then different after. Here was an honest look at friends and families in small-town America. Although Valley Stream, Long Island, is a long way from Texas, I felt like I knew those people. After seeing that film, I knew those were the kinds of stories I've always responded to and those would be the kinds of stories I would like to tell. But the dream of becoming a screenwriter still wasn't born.

My eyes opened wider after seeing François Truffaut's *The 400 Blows.* I had never seen a film like this. Again, I found myself relating to the story and falling in love with the honest approach to the storytelling. That put me on a Truffaut kick. *The Man Who Loved Women, Stolen Kisses, The Woman Next Door,* and *Day for Night* all reminded me of what I loved about Woody, the delicate balance in tone between drama and comedy. After immersing myself in these films, something else happened. I was no longer thinking about writing novels or short stories. I was thinking about writing films. I was thinking about becoming a screenwriter.

So I called my dad and told him that I wanted to write movies. We talked it out. I told him about the movies and filmmakers that were turning me on and that I really felt like I had to make movies. A few days later, he sent me the book *Screenplay: The Foundations of Screenwriting.* That was my dad; if we wanted to do something, he supported the effort.

So I found myself with this book, and the next step was up to me. I had no idea then, but this Syd Field how-to is the bible for every aspiring screenwriter, and for good reason. It tells you exactly how to do it. It delivers on the promise of the title.

I had never even seen a screenplay before, but the format I saw in the book excited me; it seemed within my grasp. It was all dialogue. I loved writing dialogue. I would finish a chapter, process the information I'd read, and say to myself, "Okay, I can do this."

FILM SCHOOL

That summer, I went to the video store every day and rented movies. I watched with a new attention to detail and determination to learn. *Mean Streets,* Martin Scorsese's first full-length film, and Spike Lee's

She's Gotta Have It, another breakout first feature, spoke to me. All had a similar sensibility. They were scrappy, intimate films. They were indies before anyone coined the term *indies*.

I returned to Albany for my junior year and signed up for every film class the school offered. Before the end of the semester, I wrote my first screenplay, a semiautobiographical story about my high school basketball team. I thought it could really get made into a movie. Maybe everyone thinks that about their scripts. Why else write them?

However, my belief in this script was so strong and passionate that I didn't see any way I could hand my script off to some guy in Hollywood and let him massacre my masterpiece. (I have since reread said script, entitled *Apple Pie*, and it is no masterpiece.) He wouldn't know me. Nor could he understand my experiences. This was a passion project. I was going to have to pull a Spike Lee and learn how to make movies myself. So I began looking into film schools.

At the time, my dad, who had gone back to school and gotten his master's while still a cop, was an adjunct professor at NYU. He taught one class each semester in communications and mass media. I thought that provided me with an inside track to getting in, and I told him I wanted to transfer to NYU, like Marty and Spike, the following year and study filmmaking.

I expected him to say he'd make a few calls and see what he could do. He seemed to know everyone. Plus, he was a great dad. He was present and involved in our lives. If my brother, sister, or I had a dream, he was there to help us get closer to them. My mom was the same.

But as soon as I mentioned NYU, he said, "Look at your grades and look at my salary. And then let's rethink NYU."

After researching film programs at other city and state schools, I enrolled for my senior year at Hunter College on Manhattan's Upper East Side. Tuition was about $600 a semester. My first class was Film Directing 101, and on the first day, the professor, Everett Aison, stood in front of the class and asked which of us wanted to direct films. Everyone of course raised his or her hand.

Then he asked how many of us had any acting experience. This time no hands went up.

"How do you expect to work with actors if you have no idea what you are going to be asking of them?"

We were silent.

He had a good point.

"What we're going to do this semester is divide into groups of four and you'll create and perform a three- to four-minute play. One of you will be the director, one will be the writer, and the other two will act." The first time, I was picked as one of the actors. A classmate wrote a short five-minute piece about a young Eurotrash couple living on the Upper East Side of New York. I played Jean Paul, and the woman opposite me was Gabrielle. We rehearsed once before class, and we were pretty terrible, which is understandable since I hadn't acted since third grade. And just as I would be years later on day one of *Saving Private Ryan*, I was scared shitless. But when it was time to put the play up on its feet, something happened that will forever be a turning point to remember. About halfway through the play, I forgot I was in a classroom. I forgot about my nervousness. I forgot about everything except what I was supposed to be saying, thinking, and reacting to in that moment. In other words, I lost myself to the role and became that other person, and it was fun. I now had the acting bug.

Afterward, my classmates were generous with their praise. A few of them said I should think about doing more acting. And I did. I put myself in the first film I made, *The Shadow*, a five-minute black-and-white silent movie about a guy who leaves his Upper West Side apartment one night and is followed by a shadow that eventually kills him. Not much acting was required in that one, but I loved the process and knew I was headed in the right direction.

THIS IS WHAT I SHOULD BE DOING

I didn't do any writing until the second semester, when I finally took my first screenwriting class, and this was the next important moment for me. The professor assigned each of us to write a ten-minute film about an isolated incident. I wrote a comedic scene about a high school couple losing their virginity.

The next time the class met, the professor announced he was going to read our pieces in front of the class. It was the first time anything I'd written would be read aloud in front of people, and I was terrified. What if my script fell flat? What if no one laughed? What if it turned out I couldn't write?

All those thoughts ran through my head as I sat in the classroom waiting for the professor to read my pages. Mine was second or third in line. Hearing the title read, followed by my name, I steadied myself. The professor was a good reader; he got the voices and the rhythm. I turned my head slightly to look around and saw people paying attention. Then came the first laugh. I exhaled, feeling relief. More laughter followed. People were into the piece. I could tell they were caught up and anticipating what was going to happen next. It was one of the greatest feelings of my life, both relief and exhilaration.

To this day I can remember exactly where I was sitting in that classroom and can hear myself say, "I can do this. This is what I should be doing."

For my senior project, I made my most sophisticated film yet. Titled *Hey Sco* and running thirteen minutes, it was about two nineteen-year-old dirtbag losers hanging out behind the bleachers of their old high school. As they drink beer and talk about how they

The first attempt at writing, directing, and acting:
playing the title character, Sco, wielding the murder weapon

have nothing to do, one of the guys—the character I played—who's holding a shovel but won't say why, finally reveals that he killed their mutual best friend the night before and buried him beneath the football field's fifty-yard line.

The writing of the *Hey Sco* script was originally influenced by Paddy Chayefsky's 1955 award-winning movie *Marty*, which my mom had recommended (and I now recommend to you if you haven't seen it).

The script had a lot of "Whatchya want to do, Marty?"

"I don't know. What do you want to do?"

Again, another story I could relate to and characters I felt I knew.

I figured I could make the film for about $1,000. And luckily for me, the screenplay won a $500 grant from the college, which covered half of my budget. My dad kicked in the other $500. (He still says, "Without that five hundred dollars from Hunter, where would you be?")

I had a three-man, all-student crew, and our equipment came from the school: an old 16 mm CP-16 camera and a Nagra sound-recording device. The two-man cast included myself and my friend and classmate Chris McGovern, now a New York City fireman.

We shot behind the bleachers of my high school football field over the course of one long, rainy day, and despite various technical glitches, delays from the weather, and other obstacles I can no longer remember, it was the greatest day of my life. The only part of the process that made me question my decision was syncing sound in postproduction, a process today's film students probably won't ever know. Lucky for them.

Hey Sco was shown on the local public broadcasting station as part of a student film festival. I couldn't believe it when I got the call. My work was going to be on television! I can remember thinking I had made the big time. It also screened during the Independent Feature Film Market (the IFFM), at the Angelika Film Center, the Greenwich Village art theater that I frequented. You got to screen your film if you paid a fee. I knew that people who bought indie movies as well as journalists and other filmmakers would be there, so I paid the fee and planned to launch myself as a filmmaker.

I photocopied five hundred flyers in my dad's office, featuring an image from the film and the times it would screen during the three-day event. I taped them up on every lamppost in the vicinity of the theater, all over Mercer and Houston, and then repeated the exercise every two hours because some other filmmaker would have thrown their flyers over mine. I also sent VHS copies of the movie to every producer, production company, and distributor in the phone book. My cover note explained that I had written my first screenplay, that I of course would be directing in addition to playing the lead role. (Remember when I said I was just young enough and dumb enough to not know any better?) Then I waited eagerly for people to respond. And one person did. The indie film consultant Bob Hawk. Bob came to my screening and saw some promise in my short film. Bob became a friend and a trusted advisor. Years later, when I brought *McMullen* as a work in progress to the IFFM, he passed it along to Amy Taubin of *The Village Voice*. In her IFFM wrap-up article, she mentioned *McMullen* as a title to watch.

TWO

BECOMING A WRITER

The summer before I started at Hunter, I went to work at a local TV news station, Fox 5, in New York City. It was an unpaid internship. My dad called a few people he knew and I ended up on the assignment desk that summer. When my classes started in September, they let me work around my schedule, which was a good deal for me. The work was interesting, the people were cool, and the office was off the same subway stop as Hunter.

Eventually, I moved from the assignment desk to a paying production assistant gig at another show they produced, *The Reporters*. As the job got more real, I started attending night classes at Hunter. It was my third semester and, as it turned out, my last semester.

My boss at *The Reporters* was a woman named Alison Meiseles. In charge of hiring and scheduling news crews, she took me under her wing. As a PA, you're expected to bust your ass and hope that someone notices you're working harder than everyone else, which was what happened to me when Alison took me aside and said she was moving to *Entertainment Tonight*.

"We're looking for PAs," she said. "How would you like to come over there? We can pay you eighteen thousand a year."

I didn't even have to think about it. I was making nowhere near that at Fox. I immediately said, "Absolutely. I'm there." And that was it. In three semesters, I had taken every film class at Hunter College and shot *Hey Sco*. I left nine credits shy of graduation and went to work at *Entertainment Tonight*. The production office, which also included the East Coast studio, was located on the third floor of the Paramount Building in Columbus Circle, now the Trump Hotel.

Every day I fantasized about running into one of the Paramount executives from out west, handing him my screenplay, and having my script green-lit there in the lobby. Never mind that I was in New York, not Hollywood, and the execs who ran the studio from out there rarely visited the building. If and when they did visit, I didn't know it. They weren't roaming the halls, making themselves accessible to lowly PAs.

I worked at *E.T.* for four years. Yes, four years—the equivalent of going to college all over again. Like college, some great things happened to me there. My job was to drive the van and help haul equipment to movie junkets and interviews. In between setting up the camera and the lights and then breaking them down, I listened to the interviews. The great thing about *E.T.* was that we interviewed everyone who came through town to promote their movie. I paid attention to whoever we interviewed, and absorbed everything.

I remember listening to Al Pacino talk about *Scent of a Woman*. Only a fraction of the interview made it on the air, but Al sat in the chair for an hour and gave us a master class on acting. I also

Lugging gear as a PA for *Entertainment Tonight*

remember when we interviewed Robert Rodriguez for the release of his debut feature, *El Mariachi*. We were close in age and he had done what I dreamed of doing. Rodriguez talked about his filmmaking process and it was like a motivational speech. I was getting closer to figuring out how I was going to make this crazy dream of mine a reality.

NO EMPTY HOURS

There was another great thing about working at *E.T.*: It provided me with a place to do my own work. You have to be resourceful when you're starting out, and this was a good example. On some days, I would have to show up early in the morning for an interview at the *Today* show or *Good Morning America*. We would get people as they made the rounds of interviews. But our next assignment might not be until four P.M. And so I would spend those empty hours at one of the desks in the crew room and write screenplays.

I should correct myself. There were no empty hours. I was always cranking out screenplays. Over the course of the first two or three years I was there, I wrote five or six screenplays. I was hungry. I had stuff to say. I had people in my head clamoring to get out. I also understood that if you're going to be a writer, you have to write. If you don't, it's not going to get done.

If you don't do it, that dream ain't gonna happen. And I was determined that something was going to happen for me. Why not? It was happening all around me. I saw Quentin Tarantino's *Reservoir Dogs* and was blown away. He was the guy I wanted to be: a writer-director-actor who had figured out how to get that first film made.

Suddenly, it seemed, the indie film movement was the most exciting thing to happen to American cinema since the arrival of Scorsese, Coppola, Woody Allen, and all the other greats in the late sixties and seventies. *Sex, Lies, and Videotape* had ignited the fire. Every year, another new filmmaker burst on the scene with a debut feature that was made on a shoestring budget. In 1989, Hal Hartley, a kid from Long Island, made *The Unbelievable Truth* for $75,000. A year later, Whit Stillman, another young filmmaker from New York, made *Metropolitan* for $225,000 and received an Oscar nomination for Best Screenplay. These budgets were a fraction of a typical Hollywood movie, yet their work was distributed and taken seriously.

In 1991, I saw Richard Linklater's film *Slacker*, another movie from a guy who seemed like me—a kid writing, directing, and shooting a movie about his experiences (he appeared in it), in a world that he knew and that others recognized as their world, too. I read up on it. Budget: $23,000.

The following year, 1992, *El Mariachi, Reservoir Dogs*, and Nick Gomez's *Laws of Gravity*, made for $35,000, hit theaters. I felt another jolt of immediacy. Like the five-figure budgets for *The Unbelievable Truth* and *Slacker*, $35,000 seemed within reach—much more so than if that figure had included one or two more zeros. It was exciting to see guys making small, personal films. They were released in theaters along with big Hollywood films, based on nothing more than merit, because their films were well written and featured talented up-and-coming actors.

This was about the time that I started to believe, in earnest, that I could do it. If you don't believe it, if you don't buy into the vision, you're going to have a hell of a time selling someone else on it.

Afterward, I had an epiphany. While I was convinced this kind of moviemaking was within my grasp, it dawned on me as I thought about my work that I was not writing the kind of scripts these guys were making. Their films were personal, inspired by their lives, and pulsing with the energy of a new generation. My scripts, on the other hand, were derivative. They were imitations of the filmmakers I'd studied in school. I was copying instead of creating my own path, and in the most important decision I made as a writer, especially as a young writer, I realized I had to find my own voice.

FINDING MY VOICE

This is the crossroads anyone in their early twenties or anyone thinking back on their early twenties can relate to; it's the moment when you plant a stake in the ground and decide who you are and who you want to become. At least you take a stab at it. I talk about finding my own voice. But the voice is already there. It's inside you, and what you have to do is listen. What's it saying? Which way is it telling you to turn?

Although, in my heart, I knew something else was wrong. The problem was with the scripts themselves. They weren't that good. Something had to be wrong with my screenwriting. Simply, I hadn't yet started to write from my personal experiences.

As I thought about how to improve my writing, and especially how to make it more original, more mine, I saw an ad for the Robert McKee class in story structure. McKee was a well-known writing instructor specializing in scriptwriting and, more specifically, in the tectonics of writing a screenplay, the nuts and bolts of its structure. His three-day course met in the auditorium at the Fashion Institute of Technology on Seventh Avenue and 26th Street, and it turned out to be the game changer for me.

It was now 1993 and I was a full-fledged movie junkie. My life was 100 percent film. I watched movies I needed to watch to further my education as a filmmaker and a fan. I read books on filmmakers. I worked at a job where we interviewed actors and directors, and I wrote scripts in my spare time. It consumed me. So sitting in a room for three solid days, listening to McKee deconstruct scripts and discuss screenplay structure and form, was my idea of heaven. I now know that some people take exception to McKee's theories on structure, but I found it extremely helpful.

In addition to explaining traditional Hollywood story structure, probably the most important thing McKee said that weekend was "For your first screenplay, what I'm going to ask all of you is to think about your favorite films and what genre they are. Whatever that genre is, I want you to write that kind of script. If you don't like murder mysteries, don't write murder mysteries." He wasn't sug-gesting we copy our favorite films or filmmakers. He was telling us to identify what kind of movie we liked and to write that kind of movie. To do what felt natural and, who knows, maybe even enjoy the process.

When I thought about what films I loved the most, I instantly knew the answer: Woody Allen movies. So I said to myself, "All right, I'm going to write whatever that genre is; whatever Woody's genre is, that's what I'm going to write."

Unlike Woody, though, I added, "I'm also going to try and write a film that I can make for twenty-five thousand dollars."

Those were my two goals.

I knew I wanted to make a personal film. Like the other indie filmmakers who had come up before me, I knew I had to tell a story that was specific and unique. I had to take the audience to a place they wouldn't necessarily know if not for my film. I also wanted to address a peeve I had with most contemporary movies I was seeing. At that time, few of the movies I saw featured guys my age who talked the way my friends and I talked. I didn't identify with anyone. No one seemed like a real person. My buddies and I talked and related to one another a certain way, and I didn't hear that from people on the screen.

I knew I wrote pretty good dialogue, so I thought, all right, I know my movie is going to be about guys around my age, with affinities and situations like me and the people I know.

In fact, my brother, Brian, played a part in my search for inspiration. We are very close, only thirteen months apart, and we are regular guys. But over a couple of beers, we would drop our guards and have honest conversations about women. It wasn't just "Hey, I want to get laid." It was more "I think I might love this woman" or "I'm afraid of getting married someday."

I had a few friends like that, too. Tough guys who, at the end of the night, when it was just the two of us sitting at the bar, were able to set aside all the macho stuff and have a real heartfelt conversation about being heartbroken over the girl who'd just broken up with him.

With those images in mind, I began to take notes, thinking about both story and budget. I figured a romantic story that revolved around the city I loved would be a good place to start. No expensive stunts or gunplay, just some guys trying to talk to some cute girls walking down some of my favorite streets in NYC. But I wanted to tell it in an authentic male voice. The guys weren't the kind you saw in a Woody Allen film. Nor were they like the guys in other big Hollywood romantic comedies. For lack of a better description, I imagined them as guys like my friends and me, regular ball-busting neighborhood guys who spend most of their time talking about girls. In fact, that's what I wrote down on a note card: GUYS TALKING ABOUT GIRLS. It was simple, timeless, and it encompassed everything I knew was important, since, as I was well aware, everything in a young man's life relates to girls.

With that in mind, I began to ask myself, "So what is this movie beyond that? What is going to help this little twenty-five-thousand-dollar indie stand out in the crowd? What else can I bring to it that will give the specificity I know it needs?"

Then one day it hit me. What was it about *The Last Picture Show* and *Marty* and *The 400 Blows* that made me want to be a filmmaker in the first place? They were honest. They felt like they were written by people who had lived those stories. Then I thought about the story I had lived.

The Irish Americans were a big part of New York culture. They were an important voice in the life of the city. Certainly they were important in my New York City. And having grown up in a tight-knit Irish American family, surrounded by similar families, my world revolved around this community and culture.

I said to myself, "That's what I'm going to write. These guys are going to be Irish. And they're not going to be just passively Irish. I'm going to make them aggressively, nostalgically Irish."

The sudden clarity I had was stunning. Woody Allen wrote and directed films about the Jewish American New York experience; Martin Scorsese wrote and directed films about the Italian American New York experience; and Spike Lee was writing and directing films about the African American New York experience. All these guys had carved their own niche. I had been asking what mine would be. Now I knew.

As soon as I said that, I knew my characters. I didn't know the story yet. But I knew the guys—and the girls. And their parents. And where they lived. And how they spent their time. And what they talked about at dinner.

And that's where I started.

THREE
THE BROTHERS McMULLEN

When I sat down to write the script for *The Brothers McMullen*, I knew I had to keep my budget in mind. I was going to write a screenplay that I could shoot as inexpensively as possible. Which meant this story would be a contemporary tale with no car chases, shoot-outs, or large party scenes with hundreds of extras. In order to keep the cost down, I knew I would need to find locations I could get for free. So before I started to write, I made a list of these locations. The first, and most obvious to me, was my parents' house. It would serve as the primary location and I figured, regardless of how long the shoot went on, they were never going to kick me out. And my mother may even cook for the cast and crew. Which she did.

From having made student films in New York City, I also knew that I could shoot in any city park for free, and though shooting on the sidewalks and streets required a permit, I knew I could get by without one if our crew was small and we worked fast. If a cop did stop us and ask for our permits, I would just drop my father's name. It had gotten me out of a few traffic tickets, and I figured it would get us a pass if we got hassled while shooting. Luckily for us, the cops in New York have more important things to worry about and we were never questioned.

You'll notice the couples in *The Brothers McMullen* never go on a date inside a restaurant or a movie theater. Those locations cost money. However, the streets in the West Village, where I lived, various park benches in Central Park and Washington Square Park, and the sidewalks of the Upper West Side were all free of charge. That's why everyone is out on the street. We didn't have access to interiors.

The scene with my agent and me walking out of a restaurant is a classic. We couldn't afford to shoot in the restaurant, so I designed a long lens shot where we parked the camera across the street. Me and Peter Johansen, another *E.T.* buddy of mine playing the part of the agent, then stepped into the restaurant and did a five-count. This gave Dick Fisher, our director of photography, an opportunity to roll the camera, and then we walked outside delivering our dialogue. We were able to get about four takes before the restaurant got wise to us. Which was all we needed. If you want to make low-budget movies, you've got to be willing to do things like that.

But I'm getting ahead of myself.

I had compiled an extensive list of possible shooting locations during my long walks through the city. Most weekends, all I did was walk around, since I had no money and couldn't afford to do much of anything else. I would cover a different neighborhood every weekend. Many nights, I would head out of my apartment at one in the morning and walk for hours, all the while making mental notes, not just locations but story ideas as well. There probably isn't a sidewalk

Shooting *The Brothers McMullen* with our bare-bones crew in Central Park

in NYC that I haven't explored. I still do my walks now, and the city never fails to inspire.

I also knew from my film school days that when you are asking actors to work for free, there is no guarantee they will show up when you need them. There is also a very good chance that, in the event they get a paying gig, you will lose them. Knowing that, I figured I should write an ensemble piece. I knew one part of my story would be my three McMullen boys and their lives at home in their childhood house, but I decided to give each one a Long Island and a New York City subplot. If for any reason one or several of my actors bailed on me, or we ran out of money, I would at least have some footage for a short film. I was being a realist. I knew the odds of getting this film made were against me.

Knowing I was going to use my parents' house, I finally zeroed in on the idea of three adult brothers forced for various reasons to move back into their father's home together.

As soon as I came up with that, I knew it was a good one-liner. I was getting there.

Robert McKee, in his class, had emphasized the value of outlining your story before you write it. He said you should outline and outline and outline, and then when you come up with the last element of the story, the script will pour out of you. He was right.

Writing was a breeze. I banged out that first draft in a few weeks. Because of all the time I spent outlining, and because I was finally writing a personal story, I never needed to stop and wonder who these characters were and what motivated them. I knew them and their world inside and out. All I had to do was type. And sometimes, they took me in a direction I didn't anticipate. It's a great feeling when the story dictates to you where it wants to go. One such scene that wasn't in my outline was the inciting incident (the event in a story's plot that catalyzes the hero to take action): After burying her husband of thirty-five years, the mother of the McMullen family moves to Ireland to be with the man she always really loved, leaving her grown-up children confused and having to figure out their own lives and romantic relationships.

FADE IN.

EXT. CALVARY GRAVEYARD (QUEENS, NY)—DAY

A gray day. The crowd from the funeral has cleared out. MRS. McMULLEN, dressed in black, pulls her son BARRY aside.

MRS. McMULLEN
Finbar, come here . . .

BARRY
Come on, Ma, don't call me Finbar, all right?

MRS. McMULLEN
Finbar, I'm telling you because you're the only one who'll understand, so you'll have to tell your brothers.

BARRY
Understand what? What's going on?

MRS. McMULLEN
I'm leaving.

BARRY
What do you mean you're leaving?

WRITING AND BUDGETING

During the writing of *McMullen*, I was living with my girlfriend, Maxine Bahns, in a one-room, rent-controlled apartment on Bank Street in the Village. We were in a great neighborhood but a shithole of an apartment. We had mice and rats, and when you turned on the light in the kitchen, hundreds of cockroaches would scatter in all directions. And still I loved it. I couldn't help but romanticize it. I wasn't working on the Great American Novel, but I was a struggling writer living in the crammed Greenwich Village apartment. I was all in.

Maxine was going for her master's degree in the classics and had her head in the books 24/7, and I think her discipline rubbed off on me. Given our close quarters, I couldn't exactly turn on the TV when she was learning how to read Greek and Latin. So if she was working, which was all the time, I worked, too.

I had a small desk and a computer that I had to fire up with two six-inch floppy discs. If you're of a certain age, you don't know what I'm talking about and should consider yourself lucky. I can't tell you how many pages I lost to corrupted floppy discs.

Being a green screenwriter, the minute that first draft of *McMullen* was done, I thought it was done. Done as in brilliant, let's shoot it. It was 130 pages—in other words, way too long. As people read the script, they responded to the same thing; the script worked best when the story focused on the three brothers hanging out together. I recognized I was skilled in handling that kind of dialogue, those types of relationships, and so I went back into the script multiple times and honed the story around them.

The script wasn't as polished as I would make it today, but I was champing to make my movie. I found a budget for Nick Gomez's movie *Laws of Gravity* published in *Filmmaker* magazine and I used that as my model.

First up, I had to find someone who was willing to shoot the film for free. A cameraman I worked with at *E.T.*, a guy named Dick Fisher, was tired of shooting news and wanted to get back to shooting film, which he'd done as a younger guy.

"If I can shoot it, I'll buy a sixteen-millimeter camera," he said.

I stuck out my hand.

"We've got a deal."

Basically, I knew I would be working with a five-man crew, tops. We needed a camera assistant, sound mixer, and two PAs to help with everything else. The problem was, I was going to have to find people to work for free. Fortunately, I had a lot of friends at *E.T.* and almost all volunteered to help when they could.

After I felt confident that I had a script and crew in place, I went to my dad and said, "All right, this is what I want to do. I am going to make this movie for twenty-five grand." Supportive, he suggested creating a limited partnership to raise the funds. We decided on five shares at $5,000 a pop and immediately got $5,000 from a friend of my father's who worked on Wall Street.

"I'll give you another five," my dad said.

However, after that initial $10,000 investment, we had trouble raising any more money. Undeterred, I told my dad that I'd use that ten grand to shoot some scenes for a great-looking trailer that we could use to raise the rest of the money. But I had no intention of making only a trailer. Once out there with a camera and actors, I was going to shoot as much of the movie as possible, if not all of it.

As I said, with no guarantee that actors would show up, I knew that I could at least count on myself to be there. That's one reason I cast myself as the middle brother. Given that I had very little acting experience (about seven days total on the various short films I had made), I wrote toward what I thought were my strengths as an actor, which was essentially playing a version of myself.

CASTING

To cast the rest of the movie, I placed an ad in *Backstage* magazine, featuring breakdowns for the main characters and the gist of what I was up to: "Low-budget, non-SAG movie seeking Irish-American actors. No pay. Will provide lunch." I gave my parents' address on Long Island; within a week, I received fifteen hundred head shots and résumés. That's another great thing about making movies in New York. We've got no shortage of hungry actors.

For the first round of auditions, I rented a rehearsal stage on 72nd Street for a half day. I think it cost two hundred bucks. And the first person through the door was Mike McGlone, who, of course, ended up playing Patrick McMullen, the younger brother to my character, Barry McMullen.

His audition blew me away. I thought this was going to be easy. The first guy to read for us nails it. But I thought, "I can't cast the very first guy that I've ever auditioned in my life." So we continued looking, and after a month of auditioning people I still hadn't cast that part and no one had come close to McGlone's audition. Then one morning I was on the subway heading to work, and McGlone got on the train and sat next to me. It was totally random. He was on his way uptown, too.

"Hey, how you doing?" he said.

I was slow to respond. I was trying to place him.

"You don't remember me," he said. "I'm Mike McGlone. I auditioned for you. The *McMullen* project."

"Ah, I didn't recognize you," I said.

"So what's happening with the movie?" he asked.

In that instant, I decided to cast him.

"You know, it's funny," I said. "You got the part."

The next key bit of casting was Connie Britton, who had also sent us her head shot. By the time she auditioned, we had seen a number of actresses read for the part of Molly, and I was worried. I started to think that maybe my script stunk because each time someone read for the part, the scene fell flat. And then Connie came in. After her first take, I thought, oh, okay, this is how an actor does it.

Shortly after, we cast Shari Albert as Susan, Elizabeth McKay in the role of Ann, and my girlfriend, Maxine Bahns, to play the part of Audrey. Through Mike, we found Jennifer Jostyn, who played Leslie. They were waiters together in a restaurant. We auditioned Jennifer at Mike's apartment and cast her immediately. But there was one part we couldn't cast, that of the oldest brother, Jack McMullen. Part of the reason was that we were doing a non-SAG movie and it's hard to find good actors in their thirties. You can find young up-and-comers like McGlone and Connie Britton, who hadn't gotten into the union yet. But when you're pushing thirty, you're either good enough to be in the union or you've given up the dream.

Then I remembered I had played softball a couple of years earlier with a big, burly Irish guy named Jack Mulcahy, an actor who looked the way I imagined the Jack in my script. Through some mutual friends, I tracked him down, had him read, and he was perfect—and available.

So now I had the cast. We were ready to shoot.

SHOOTING

Remember, in theory, I was supposed to shoot a few scenes and put together a promotional reel we could use to raise the rest of the money we needed to make the movie. In practice, I was hell-bent on getting as much of this film done as possible.

The first thing I did was reenroll in one class at Hunter College so that I was eligible for the student discount when buying film for our shoot. To save even more money, I bought recanted 16 mm film stock. These were short rolls of film that were left over from music video and commercial shoots. It was a gamble because you had no guarantee that the camera assistant who put the unused film back in the can hadn't exposed it, but what choice did we have? Again. You do what you got to do.

We started in October and over the course of three months, we shot a total of six full days and got a good chunk of the script on film. The uninitiated might ask, Why only six days? Simple. When you have a cast and crew of people who have full-time jobs and are working for free in their spare time, it's nearly impossible to coordinate times when everyone is available. If my director of photography had to work on a weekend, we couldn't shoot. If one of my actors had an audition or had to cover for someone at their paying jobs, we couldn't shoot. If one of the five guys who jumped in to be our sound mixer wasn't available, we couldn't shoot. But some of those weren't even a full day of shooting. There were days at *Entertainment Tonight* when I would look at the assignment board, see we were going to finish at two o'clock, and then round up whoever I could. "All right, we got that scene between Patrick and Susan in Central Park. I'll call to see if they can get out of work this afternoon." So I'd call McGlone and Shari Albert. "Dick and I are free. We'll meet you on the corner of Seventy-second and Central Park West and shoot the breakup scene."

Often, I would write new scenes for whoever was available. I rewrote constantly. It was the kind of thing you do when you don't know any better, and being a twenty-five-year-old kid who'd never made a film, I was flying by the seat of my pants. I had no idea how movies got made. I just wanted to get mine made.

For a first-timer, I was pretty confident on set. I felt I was good at working with the actors and I knew my script and how I wanted it to sound. But I wasn't sure about how I wanted it to look. And because of that, each night before shooting, I would lie in bed, worried about where to put the camera in the next day's scene. *They are sitting at a table, someone walks into the room . . . how do I do that again?*

I got into this as a writer, not as a guy who loved the camera. I didn't sit in the theater and fall in love with how Scorsese moved the camera through the Copa, although I certainly appreciated it; instead, I fell in love with the acting and the dialogue in *Goodfellas*. My thing was always dialogue. I wanted to write the great lines, the lines people would tell their friends the next day, like Woody and Billy Wilder. I was never like most of my peers who fell in love with certain shots and obsessed about wanting to execute the cool shots they saw in classic movies.

So what did I do? I turned to Woody again. I would take out a

VHS copy of *Annie Hall* or *Manhattan* or *Hannah and Her Sisters*, turn off the volume, watch scenes, and take notes. *Annie walks through the door and into the kitchen. Alvy is already there, waiting for her. They sit down and talk. Alvy gets up, the camera stays on her, the single is on Alvy; he carries something back to the table.*

Okay, I would think, that's how you do this scene. I know what we're doing tomorrow.

In any event, I was happy with the footage we got those first six days. But by January 1993, we ran low on cash, were hit by a number of snowstorms, and Dick Fisher herniated a disk in his back. Production screeched to a halt and we didn't shoot for more than two months. To keep my cast engaged, I made sure we continued to meet every couple of weeks to rehearse at Jack's apartment. These were invaluable sessions for two reasons. One, the cast was becoming a tight-knit bunch, a family of sorts, and second, the script was getting better, the scenes crisper. But after two months of not shooting, the actors, understandably, got antsy. And then, all of a sudden, it seemed as if the production was over.

It was March, and I was at *Entertainment Tonight* when Dick approached me with awful news. He was ready to bail.

I refused to let him quit. If he left . . . well, I wasn't going to allow that to happen.

"Look, I'll give you a big chunk of this movie if you will just finish this film," I said. "You can become a full partner with me here. But we've come too far. We're doing good work. Help me get to the end."

Fortunately, Dick said, "Okay, let's do it."

As spring approached, I knew I had to get this film done as quickly as possible. I couldn't keep asking my actors, Dick, and friends to work for free. My folks had just about had it with me shooting in every room of their house. So I asked my dad for another $2,000 and I chipped in whatever money I was making at *E.T.* At this point, I knew we could no longer afford to process the film, so all the money went to buying film stock and pizza. I had forty pages of the script still left to shoot and I was determined to get those scenes in the can. Over the next two months, we shot another six days. I didn't worry about how I was going to pay for the film processing. I figured I would cross that bridge when we came to it.

I used the same film lab, DuArt on 55th Street, that I had used for all my student films. The man who owned the lab, Irwin Young, was sympathetic to the struggles of young filmmakers. He was an enthusiastic supporter of indie film and was always willing to help. Hearing that his partner, Bob Smith, was a big fan of the NYPD, my dad visited the lab and worked out an arrangement with Irwin and Bob. "Whatever we end up owing you," he said, "I give you my word that you will get paid back."

And that was enough for Irwin and Bob. There was no contract, just a handshake. DuArt agreed to defer the processing costs, almost $12,000, and develop the film so I could get started in the editing room.

Nobody makes a film alone. Without the support of those two men, my parents, and the cast and crew who were willing to work for free, I don't have this story to tell.

FOUR

THE TWELVE GREATEST DAYS OF MY LIFE

*E*ntertainment Tonight had Beta editing machines, so Dick Fisher and I had the film transferred to Beta and edited the film at night. At the end of the workday, we went downstairs and had a drink at a nearby bar. Then, after everyone had cleared out of the office, we went back up, turned the handle on a side door we'd left open, and worked until four in the morning.

Eventually, we had a two-hour rough cut. The film didn't have a finished sound mix, and at the time, the music we had temped in, traditional Irish folk music by a young composer named Seamus Egan, hadn't been cleared, but I felt the movie was ready to show to the world. I took the Beta master and had copies transferred to VHS. I sent them out, along with a letter, to every film festival in North America, every distribution company (Miramax, Fine Line, October

Films, etc.), and every manager and agent who represented an independent writer or director.

I was comprehensive, thorough, detail-oriented, and driven.

My goal was simple. I needed an agent. I wanted representation.

I thought if these people could see my film, they would say, at the worst, we can't do anything with this tiny movie but the kid's a writer and a director and an actor; we'll sign him.

So that was my goal: Get *McMullen* seen and get signed.

Within a month, though, the rejection letters started coming in. I didn't even get a nibble from an agent, a manager, or a film festival. Nothing. I was a dead fish in still water. The final straw came when I received a turndown from the Hamptons International Film Festival. I was a Long Island filmmaker. *McMullen* was a Long Island movie. The Hamptons festival was brand-new. And they rejected my movie?

Needless to say I was pissed off, an angry young man, feeling sorry for himself. I had done the impossible. It had taken me three years to write a script, find the money, and make the movie, and nobody gave a shit. That's when my dad interceded and took me out for a drink. We went to the White Horse Tavern down the block from my apartment in the Village. He listened to me bitch and moan about what had happened with the movie after I sent it out— or, more accurately, what hadn't happened. In the midst of my depressing monologue, he told me to shut up. Which I did. He then asked me:

"After you finished shooting your film, do you remember what you said to me? You told me, 'Shooting *Brothers McMullen* was the twelve greatest days of my life.'"

"And they were," I said.

"Well, did you make this film because you wanted to become rich and famous?"

I shook my head.

"Did you make the film because you wanted to go out to Hollywood, chase girls, and be an asshole?"

No.

"As I recall, you made this film because you had something to say and because this is what you want and need to do with your life."

I nodded.

"Then stop complaining, sit down, and write another screenplay," he said. "We'll figure out a way to get you another twenty-five thousand dollars and get you another twelve days. We'll keep grabbing those twelve days every couple of years until this thing *does* happen for you."

And that's what I set out to do. I figured I could probably make three more low-budget twelve-day movies before I was thirty-five. If it didn't happen for me by then, well, at least I gave it a real shot. Besides, what was the alternative? Making movies wasn't a job I was looking to get; making movies was now who I was.

There was one more festival where I could submit my film, and that was the Sundance Film Festival, founded by Robert Redford and his production company in Utah. I knew this was the most prestigious film festival for independent filmmakers, and the application deadline was coming up. The reason I hadn't applied? Money.

I think the submission fee was a couple of hundred bucks, and I didn't want to spend another cent on this film. I hadn't paid my rent in almost six months, my credit cards were maxed out, and we were in the hole $12,000. Even so, something told me that I had to find a way to send in my film, that this was the one. So I scrounged up the dough, dropped the envelope in the mail, and waited.

Again, nothing happened.

In September 1994, the movie *Quiz Show* was released. Redford had produced, directed, and also starred in this movie based on the TV quiz show scandal of the 1950s. I was part of the *Entertainment Tonight* crew covering the movie's press junket, which included Redford. Desperate, I decided to make my own break. I went to my boss, Vincent Rubino, who was producing the junket, and said, "Look, I want to give Redford a VHS copy of my movie."

Being a friend, Vin just said, "Do what you want, but I never heard what you just said and I don't know a thing about it."

The next day we were interviewing Redford in a hotel room. As the production assistant, I was next to the camera, standing only a few feet from the superstar actor-director-producer as he answered questions. Yet I didn't hear a word he said. Instead of listening, I was rehearsing what I was going to say as I handed him a copy of my movie. I had memorized a ninety-second pitch and knew I would be lucky if he gave me even that much time.

As soon as he finished the interview, Redford went out the door to the elevator. I immediately bolted out another door and met him there. He was with his publicist. Holding the VHS cassette of my film in my hand, I made my pitch. "I'm an independent filmmaker, and this movie I just made is great. It's not finished. I still need finishing funds. Maybe the Sundance Institute could help. Or maybe it's right for the festival. Regardless, I would appreciate it if you could take a look at it."

Redford took the tape, thanked me, and stepped into the elevator. As the doors closed, I saw him hand it to his publicist. Then they were gone.

Two months later, in November, I received a letter from the Sundance Institute, turning down my request for funds to help finish my film. They wished me luck. To me, the letter was a sign I needed to move on. I had been a production assistant at *Entertainment Tonight* for four years and probably overstayed my welcome by about three years. I needed to make more money and start charting a path toward a real career.

I put together a clip reel of scenes from *McMullen* and prepared letters to E!, VH1, MTV, and other cable networks, introducing myself as someone who could direct bumpers[1] between shows and work my way up. I was a week away from mailing this when I arrived one morning at the *E.T.* offices and found a phone message from Geoff Gilmore, the director of the Sundance Film Festival.

I immediately called him back.

"I have the VHS tape of your movie and it says this is a rough cut. Have you finished it yet?"

"Yes, it's finished," I replied.

I was lying. It wasn't finished.

"What's the running time now?" he asked.

In reality, it was two hours.

"About ninety minutes," I said.

"What scenes did you cut out?" he asked.

I mentioned a handful of scenes that I wanted to cut or thought could be cut.

"That's great," Gilmore said. "I'm happy to hear that. We'll give you a call in a few days."

A few days later, *The Brothers McMullen* was officially accepted into the Sundance Film Festival. I was stunned as I hung up the phone. It was fantastic news—except for the fact that I had only two months to finish the film. And I was broke.

---

1 Bumpers: short clips that appear between the show and the commercials.

SUNDANCE INSTITUTE

September 21, 1994

[illegible]

Dear Mr. Burns,

Your film was forwarded onto our office from Mr. Redford's office. Unfortunately the Sundance Insitute does not provide finishing funds for incompleted films.

I have enclosed information on the support the Institute does provide and should you be interested in one of our programs, please feel free to apply with the application enclosed.

I wish you the best of luck in completing your project *The Brothers McMullen* and am sorry we couldn't get back to you sooner.

Sincerely,

Michelle Satter
Director
Feature Film Program

UTAH: P.O. BOX 16450 SALT LAKE [illegible]
CALIFORNIA: 225 SANTA MONICA BOULEVARD 8TH FLO[illegible]

SUNDANCE INSTITUTE

December 1, 1994

Dear Filmmaker:

Congratulations on your film being selected to screen at the 1995 Sundance Film Festival.

As the director of your film, you are responsible for ensuring your print is shipped to the Festival in accordance with our instructions. You are also entitled to special benefits including complimentary transportation, lodging, and a package of tickets to screenings, panel discussions, and special events.

Enclosed please find important information regarding your participation at the Festival. Please plan carefully. Once you have selected your dates and have been ticketed, we will not be able to accommodate any changes.

We look forward to meeting you in January!

Sincerely,

Coleen Reardon
Assistant Managing Director

Jill Miller
Associate Managing Director

UTAH: P.O. BOX 16450 SALT LAKE CITY UTAH 84116 TEL 801 328 3456 FAX 575 5175
CALIFORNIA: 225 SANTA MONICA BOULEVARD 8TH FLOOR SANTA MONICA CALIFORNIA 90401 TEL 310 394 4662 FAX 394 8353

Sundance rejection and acceptance letters

GETTING READY FOR SUNDANCE

Through his job as the NYPD's media spokesman, my dad knew a number of journalists and some television news executives. He gave a VHS cassette of *The Brothers McMullen* to one of these friends, David Evans, an Aussie who was running FX at the time. Evans watched the movie, loved it, and decided to help out. He said that on his next trip to LA, he would get the film to Tom Rothman. Tom was a smart young movie executive who had left the Samuel Goldwyn Company to start Fox's new indie label, Fox Searchlight.

Rothman was so new he didn't even have an office. Nor did he have a budget for his company. As he later recalled, though, a man with an Australian accent tracked him down, handed him my movie, and said he needed to watch it.

Having been on the job for a week, Rothman figured when an Australian on the Fox lot asks you to watch a movie, you should watch the movie. Rothman did—and dug it. However, his new company wasn't picking up any films yet.

Instead, he put me in touch with indie film veterans Ted Hope and James Schamus, who ran a production company in New York called Good Machine. Ted and James came on as executive producers, with the express goal of helping me finish the movie.

Rothman also introduced me to John Sloss, an attorney who represented all the important names in independent film: John Sayles, Richard Linklater, Todd Haynes. Hearing that Sloss worked with Sayles was enough for me. I had seen Sayles speak, back in film school. One of my heroes, he made personal films that he wrote, directed, and acted in. Sloss was also a basketball fanatic like me. The decision was easy. I wanted John Sloss to represent me, too. I've been working with John for twenty years now and he remains one of my best friends and most trusted advisor.

After seeing *McMullen*, Sloss agreed to help sell it. He went back to Rothman at Fox Searchlight, who wasn't acquiring films yet, but he gave us the $50,000 we needed to finish in exchange for a deal that gave him the first look. We needed the $25,000 to finish cutting the film and another $25,000 to blow the film up from 16 mm to 35 mm.

Needing to get the film done by January, life turned into a blur. After a full day at *Entertainment Tonight*, I would head to the editing room to finish *McMullen*. There was barely time to sleep. As I struggled to cut the last ten minutes, Ted Hope advised me to be fearless. "No one," he said, "has ever walked out of a movie and said, 'God, that was a great movie, but it was too short.' We all talk about the ten minutes in the middle where it dragged."

I knew he was right, but I also remembered what it cost to shoot those scenes he wanted to cut, not just the monetary cost but the begging and pleading and planning that went into every shooting day. But he persisted.

"Look, if these scenes that are painful to cut are any good, you'll put them in your next screenplay," he said.

Thinking that made sense, I made the cuts and got the running time down to ninety minutes. And you know, none of those scenes I cut ever ended up in another screenplay. The scenes you cut deserve to be cut.

James Schamus also gave me crucial advice. It was mid-December, about a month before we were heading to Sundance, and he said, "I don't know what is going to happen with *The Brothers McMullen* at Sundance. But I can tell you that the two weeks you're there will be the hottest you will ever be in your career. You need to have another

Me and postproduction supervisor Bill Baldwin cutting *McMullen* late into the night, trying to finish the film in time for Sundance

screenplay ready so that when you're in a meeting and someone asks what you want to do next, you can put a screenplay down in front of them and say, 'This is my next film.' And it's very likely, if things play out in your favor, that it will get green-lit right there."

I went home that night and started to write a new script. I had been toying with the idea of writing more of a straight comedy, something with an exaggerated reality and characters. At the time, I was on a Neil Simon kick, and I had recently watched *Barefoot in the Park*. I had also just rewatched *Moonstruck* and decided I wanted to try my hand at something that was tonally similar to those films. I decided to write a funny version of *McMullen*, which I called *The Fighting Fitzpatricks* (and later retitled *She's the One*).

I banged it out in four weeks. I replaced the oldest brother with a dad and wrote specifically for McGlone and Maxine, both of whom were in *McMullen* with me. I didn't worry about the similarities between the two movies because I didn't think anyone would see *McMullen* after it screened at Sundance. All I knew was, I had to have a finished script when I went to the festival. And I did.

SUNDANCE

I arrived at Park City three days before the film got there. It was still being processed at the lab and showed up only when Ted Hope brought it with him on the plane from New York the day of the screening. I still had not seen the film projected in a theater. My first time would be our first screening at the Egyptian Theatre on Main Street. The packed audience included Sloss and all the buyers. As the house lights dimmed, I watched my title sequence come up in front of three hundred people. Then during the first scene, people laughed and continued to laugh. The movie was working, but I must have looked like a nervous wreck because an elderly woman sitting next to me grabbed my arm and said, "Relax, honey, they like it."

A moment later, I saw Sloss bolt out of the screening and go to the lobby. He sensed the buzz starting; indeed, the buyers loved the film and he got himself in position to deal with all the inquiries. Film deals, like politics, are all about back-room and behind-the-scenes relationships. Miraculously, the pieces were falling into place.

After the movie ended, I was invited onstage for a Q&A. The

moderator invited people to stay if they wanted to meet me, and a long line snaked out the back door. I spoke to everyone. They were actors, filmmakers, agents, producers, and distributors. All offered congratulations. Some said they wanted to represent me. Others said they wanted to produce my next movie. I got invites to "do lunch" next time I was in LA. They all handed me their business cards and later I took them back to New York and compared them against the rejection letters I had gotten for the film when I'd first sent it out. This was especially helpful when trying to decide which agent I would later sign with.

Before the second screening at Sundance, Tom Rothman said he wanted to buy the movie. We had a few other offers, but I knew the honorable thing was to sell the movie to Fox Searchlight since they had given us the money to finish the film. However, Miramax's chief, Harvey Weinstein, had yet to arrive at the festival and he sent word that he didn't want us to sell the movie without letting him see it first.

I couldn't believe it. Harvey Weinstein was going to be upset if he didn't get to see my film? This was heady stuff. Still, we all felt that we should go with Rothman, and that's what we did.

The Brothers McMullen was the first movie sold at the festival that year, and the minute it sold, I could feel my life change. Suddenly, I was sitting down with *The New York Times*, the *Los Angeles Times*, and other papers. Everybody wanted to talk to me and the other actors in the movie. The dream was coming true. Then, as Schamus had predicted, Fox Searchlight wanted to make my next movie. I could hear his words echoing in my ears: "You'll never be hotter than those two weeks." He was right.

By this time, my brother and my parents had come out to Park City to join me. We all attended the festival's closing awards ceremony; Tom DiCillo's *Living in Oblivion* was the favorite to win Best Picture and some thought *McMullen* was going to take the Audience Award.

But *Living in Oblivion* won the Waldo Salt Screenwriting Award, and the Audience Award went to Kayo Hatta's *Picture Bride.* I assumed we were done and not going to get an award. But, hey, I'd sold the film, my next movie was already in the works, and as far as I was concerned, the festival could not have been more successful.

Then Samuel Jackson went to the podium to announce the winner of the Grand Jury Prize, the festival's top award, and with typical flourish, he filled the moment with drama before announcing the last three words I expected to hear, *The Brothers McMullen.* I was stunned. And thrilled. I was with my parents, my brother, and my cast and crew, and we were all hugging and high-fiving.

And that's the last thing I remember. I know that I walked up to the stage, gave a thank-you speech, accepted the award, and gave Sam a hug. But I was in a daze. The really crazy part is that at the after-party, at midnight, it was my birthday. I turned twenty-seven. I could not have had a better celebration. Earlier, I had done an interview with a crew from *Entertainment Tonight,* and my colleagues had asked, "Are you coming back to work?"

I laughed.

I think we all knew the answer. This was my new job. I was already at work.

FRIENDS IN HIGH PLACES

During this time, I lucked into mentors who offered counsel and advice, starting with Michael Nozik, who ran Robert Redford's company, Wildwood Enterprises. We met at Sundance after the first screening of *McMullen* through Rothman and ICM agent Bart

Walker, whom I was leaning toward signing with. Nozik and I hit it off immediately. He said, "I'm going to bring Redford by one of the next screenings. He wants to see the movie in the theater."

At the third screening, I was seated next to my parents, and just after the lights went down I got the elbow: Redford was coming in. Apparently, the last row at all the screenings was left empty in case the festival's founder wanted to drop in. Sure enough, as I turned my head slightly, just enough to see the back row out of the corner of my eye, there he was.

Afterward, Redford found me and praised the film. It was more than I'd bargained for, but I recovered enough to say, "You've got to meet my mom." Before leaving, Redford said, "We should talk," and unlike many people who said the same thing to me, he meant it.

When I returned to New York, my answering machine was full. *McMullen* had been mentioned in *Time* magazine, and I was still listed in the New York phone book. Friends, family, and people I hadn't spoken to since I was a little kid left messages congratulating me. Tons of agents, producers, and managers also called to ask when I was coming to LA.

Soon I was ensconced at the fabled Chateau Marmont hotel on the Sunset Strip, where people referred to me as Mr. Burns, and a case of Guinness beer was waiting for me in my room, compliments of Wildwood Productions. Over the next five surreal days, I met all the big muckety-mucks at the agencies and studios. Despite my inexperience, I had a pretty clear vision of my career: I wanted to be a writer-director-actor and make my small films, like Woody, and one day, if things worked out, I wanted to make my Irish American *Godfather*.

Because of the heat *McMullen* had from Sundance, I was put into bed with the best of the best. In addition to being represented by

John Sloss and working with Tom Rothman, I signed with ICM: Bart Walker and Robert Newman became my primary agents in LA, and Sam Cohn, Woody's agent, agreed to look out for me in New York. Redford came on *She's the One* as executive producer and helped serve as a godfather of sorts if I needed help with Fox, advice with my agency, some muscle in the business, or office space in LA. Redford's head of production, Michael Nozik, who had become a friend and mentor, also signed on as a producer.

It was a wild ride. One night I was having dinner with Nozik and he asked if I had any ideas for a Redford–Paul Newman movie. I pitched him a couple. Obviously, none stuck. But it was cool just to be let in on that conversation. Redford was all about staying grounded and real. I remember he said, "Look, this is a crazy business. There are going to be a lot of people who will try to take advantage of your situation. If you have a question, if you're unsure about something, the door is open. Feel free to ask me."

Having these guys in my corner was invaluable. My dad was always my go-to guy when I needed to talk something out, but Redford, Nozik, and the others offered years of experience in the business I was entering (in the most unusual way). My advice to young filmmakers: Talk to people who have been through it. Ask questions. At the end of the day, you can make the decisions, but let those with a longer résumé help you figure out the answers or at least the best possibilities. I had no idea whether I was making the right moves as I hurtled into my next project while waiting for *McMullen* to hit theaters. But I'll tell you this: One day we had a table read at Wildwood's New York offices, and I felt a comfort level I didn't have with *McMullen* when I glanced down the conference table and saw Robert Redford listening and taking notes.

FIVE
SHE'S THE ONE

Following Sundance, I hit the ground running with the script I sold to Fox Searchlight. One issue lingering in front of me as my second movie came together was the title. Early on—and I don't recall who was responsible—someone said, "We can't follow up *The Brothers McMullen* with *The Fighting Fitzpatricks*." And I agreed. So we had to find a new title.

In the meantime, I couldn't think of a better title and neither could anyone else. The studio hired an outside company to brainstorm titles. Inspired by the family's fishing trips, they suggested *Hook, Line and Sinker, Gone Fishing,* and few dozen others in that vein. Not one worked.

One day I was listening to Springsteen's *Born to Run* album. I'm a Springsteen nut and the song "She's the One" came on and it caused me to pause. Francis Fitzpatrick says at some point in the script, "I think she's the one." And his brother, Mickey, also mentions Hope being "the one" for him. It hit me then. The whole movie was about which of these girls was "the one." And so *She's the One* became the new title.

I remember sitting down with Tom Rothman to talk about the budget of *She's the One,* and saying, "I don't want to make it for any more than three million dollars." I was serious. Although I probably could have gotten the movie green-lit at $20 million, I thought it would be very difficult to make a third film if I lost someone $15 million. But if my next movie didn't work at $3 million, I wouldn't get kicked out of the business.

I had never been on a film set other than *McMullen,* where some days the entire crew was Dick Fisher and me. I didn't know what an assistant director did, and the same was true for such basics as a grip, a gaffer, and a best boy. I wasn't 100 percent sure I even knew how to make movies.

What I did know was this: I didn't want to show up on a $20 million set and be overwhelmed. I didn't want to be the phenom who was called up to the major leagues only to have everyone discover he couldn't hit a curve. A $3 million budget seemed within my realm. And really, it came down to wanting to avoid the pressure. In order to grow, I knew I had to step out of my comfort zone. But I didn't want to go so far that I couldn't handle it.

A KILLER CAST

I had never been this busy in my life. In addition to preparing *McMullen* for its theatrical release, looking for a release date, cutting a trailer, doing a photo shoot for the poster (because we didn't have any behind-the-scenes photography), and giving interviews to long-lead press, I also began preproduction on *She's the One*.

Fox Searchlight sent me looking for a director of photography. After meeting with a bunch of excellent people with both studio and indie credits, I hired Frank Prinzi. He was a New Yorker, and I wanted a New Yorker. He had also shot DiCillo's *Living in Oblivion* and I sensed our personalities meshed. That was also true with costume designer Susan Lyall, whom I still see all the time in Tribeca, and Laura Rosenthal, the first casting director I worked with.

After fifteen years assisting Woody Allen's award-winning casting director, Juliet Taylor, Laura wanted to branch off on her own, and I was thrilled to have someone on my movie who had worked so closely with one of my filmmaking idols. The process was new to me. The movie was about two Irish American brothers in New York with very different love lives and outlooks on life in general, which come into conflict and test their controlling father's sense of family and tradition. It was *McMullen* rewritten with more humor.

I knew the brothers were going to be played by Mike McGlone and me, and my real-life girlfriend, Maxine Bahns, was going to step into a similar role on-screen. The three other pivotal roles were: the father at the center of the Fitzpatrick family, McGlone's wife, and the woman McGlone cheats with—who also happens to be my character's ex-fiancée. Laura and I began talking about who would be right as the father. A bunch of names had been given to us, but she immediately mentioned John Mahoney, the actor who played Frasier's father Martin Crane on *Frasier*, and the minute she did, it was a no-brainer. He was perfect.

Looking back at this process, what's interesting is that at the time, I was rewriting the script and trying to lock in on a consistent tone. I was rewatching *Moonstruck* to see how the screenwriter, John Patrick Shanley, balanced the exaggerated characters and comedic situations with the more serious dramatic scenes. Not only is Mahoney in that Oscar-winning film, but Anita Gillette and Robert Weil are also in it, and I ended up casting all three in *She's the One.* The other key supporting part was McGlone's driver. McGlone's character was a twenty-five-year-old hotshot Wall Streeter, and he rode to work in a town car whose driver listens to his confession about the previous night. My dad said, "You've got to give that to Malachy." He was referring to Malachy McCourt, whose brother was *Angela's Ashes* author Frank McCourt. Both were members of my dad's First Friday Club, a mix of New York Irishmen who got together to drink and tell stories the first Friday of every month at different Irish bars on the Upper East Side.

That left the two leads: McGlone's wife, Renee, and the sexy woman who causes all the pain and suffering, Heather. Laura's expertise, and the benefit of a talented casting director in general, was never more evident than when we looked at actresses for these roles. Between LA and New York we auditioned, among others, Angelina Jolie, Jennifer Lopez, Heather Graham, Amanda Peet, Anne Heche, Lauryn Hill, and Jennifer Garner.

One look at that list and you see this was a magic moment in Hollywood for actresses, and whether I knew it or not was beside the point, because Laura was dialed in. Years later, Michael Nozik and I would say, "My God, it was like every girl that came through our door became a giant movie star."

Our New York auditions were in the Tribeca Film Center, which had the vibe of a hip place but was situated in what was then a ghost town.

We were very close to casting someone in the part of Renee, I won't mention who, when Jennifer Aniston became available. *Friends* had just finished its first season; I hadn't seen it yet, but Jennifer was breaking out. The challenge of casting Renee was that we needed someone who could play the New York sarcasm without coming across too tough. That nuance made a big difference.

Jennifer auditioned in the conference room at Fox Searchlight in Los Angeles. Most auditions were videotaped for second and third looks, if not comparisons, but not hers. Afterward, I looked at Tom Rothman and I said what all of us were thinking: "She's exactly what we've been looking for."

Likewise with Cameron Diaz, who played Heather. She was the only actress we saw who didn't audition. Her team said we could watch her films, meet with her, and hear what she thought about the character, but she wouldn't audition. After meeting with her, I knew she would be perfect for Heather. Rothman said, "Mark my words, that girl is going to be a huge star."

Leslie Mann and Amanda Peet rounded out the cast. Leslie was so good that I expanded the bartender role from one to multiple scenes in order to give her more to do. Then Amanda, who was raised in Manhattan and went to a posh uptown school, read for the part of Renee's sister. She came in with her hair teased, chewing gum, and speaking with a thick Long Island accent. We chatted before and after her audition, and once she left, I turned to Laura and said, "That girl is great! She's the real deal. She's like the girls I grew up with."

Laura laughed.

"That's all a put-on," she said. "That's not her accent. She's from New York City. She just graduated from Columbia University."

In spite of that pedigree, I still cast her.

I WILL REMEMBER YOU

Amid all of this, we were also finishing up our postproduction work on *The Brothers McMullen*. The folks from Fox Searchlight thought it might be helpful to have a pop song play over the tail credits of the film. I told them I was all for the idea but would have to run it by Seamus Egan, the film's music composer.

Seamus was a traditional Irish folk musician who had allowed me to use his music free of charge when it played at Sundance. After selling the film to Searchlight, we were able to finally pay Seamus for his wonderful score. When I told Seamus of Fox's idea, he was excited by the notion of it. He gave me a list of three artists who he felt might be a good fit and complement his music that we used in the film. One of the artists was Sarah McLachlan. It seemed like a long shot, but Fox approached Sarah, screened the film for her, and asked if she was interested. She was.

When Sarah saw the film, she fell in love with Seamus's instrumental cue that we used over the tail credits. She suggested writing lyrics for that song and rerecording it with vocals. That song, "Weep Not for the Memories" (later titled "I Will Remember You"), not only became *McMullen*'s tail credits song but also one of Sarah's biggest hits.

The song ultimately reached number 14 on the Billboard charts in 1999, and the live version earned Sarah a Grammy Award in 2000.

Fox Searchlight was throwing all its eggs into the *McMullen* basket because the film was their debut picture. They were not only launching a film but also launching their new specialized film division, and we benefited from that concentrated focus.

I worked tirelessly with David Dinerstein and his bare-bones staff as they created the poster, trailer, and television commercials.

They set up an exhaustive press plan that involved my spending the summer of 1995 crisscrossing the country and speaking to every newspaper journalist, radio talk-show host, and entertainment news reporter who would have me. Closer to the film's release that August, I hit the talk-show circuit in both Los Angeles and New York, doing the *Today* show, *Charlie Rose*, and *Late Night with Conan O'Brien*.

McMullen opened August 11, 1995, on seven screens with a $23,000 per screen average for the weekend. These were huge numbers, better than Fox had expected. Glowing reviews flowed in from *The Washington Post*, *USA Today*, and *The New York Times* ("a romantic comedy full of heart and humor"). The film went on to win Best First Feature at the Independent Spirit Awards and a Special Jury Prize at the Deauville Film Festival in France. *McMullen* stayed in theaters until early December, earning $10.4 million domestically.

You can't imagine the thrill I felt walking down 12th Street in the West Village and stopping in front of the Art Greenwich movie theater (now torn down and replaced by a fitness center) and seeing *The Brothers McMullen* up in lights. And the film sharing the marquee with mine? Woody Allen's *Mighty Aphrodite*. Burns and Allen. My brother took this great photo the following night.

The next month, production began on *She's the One*, and ironically, my first day of shooting was the first time I had been on a legit film set. And even more ironic, I was the guy in charge.

The scene called for my character to pull up in his cab in front of a terminal at JFK International Airport. When I arrived on set that morning, I couldn't believe the size of the crew and the number of trucks lined up alongside the curb. Equipment filled the sidewalk. People were going in and out of the makeup trailers. And everybody there was looking at me to tell them what we were going to do.

Truth be told, I was shitting my pants. Think about it: I had gone from making a movie in my mom's kitchen to having part of the United Airlines terminal closed. On *McMullen*, no one was behind me when I called action. On *She's the One*, I turned around and saw an army.

However, once the day started, I realized that between "action" and "cut," you don't think about the army. You focus only on the actors in front of the camera at that moment, and as I subsequently learned, it doesn't matter whether your film is budgeted at $3,000 or $30 million, all that counts is getting your shot.

Indeed, after that first day, I thought, okay, this is how it works on a big show, and I settled in. After that day one, I rode to work most days with producers Michael Nozik and Ted Hope and my director of photography, Frank Prinzi. While driving, the four of us would break down the day. We would discuss the day's goals, what we needed to accomplish, and the challenges we thought we would face. I still do that today with my producer and DP. That drive to set always reminds me of a pregame locker room pep talk.

There were some things I had to get used to, working on a "proper" film. I had trouble getting used to going into hair and makeup. Since I still didn't think of myself as an actor, that interruption always struck me as odd, and I looked forward to the days when I didn't work in front of the camera because then I wouldn't have to leave the set. Other changes also took some getting used to. For instance, I had a full crew, a great team that could do almost anything I asked. Not that I was looking to do anything too sophisticated. But if we wanted me and Mike to do a long walk and talk through Battery Park, we could lay down track and keep us in focus.

We also had the money to dress a location. McGlone's and Aniston's characters, Francis and Renee, could afford a nice place, and so we went all over the city looking for a great loft. When we found one,

On the set of *She's the One*, shooting in one of the local hangouts,
Tortilla Flats, in the West Village

the production designer said, "All right, this is great. Now I want to replace all of the furniture, paint the wall, and wax the floors." Again, this was new to me.

On *McMullen*, we didn't even think to move the couch. If the couch was against the wall, we shot the scene there. So it took some time to wrap my head around the idea that we had the money to make a location look exactly the way we wanted.

We also had the time and the money to move the camera however and wherever we wanted. Woody Allen does these great moving master shots[2] in which he essentially has a two- or three-minute scene involving two or three people in a room. Rather than shooting it in the traditional manner—a wide shot, a medium shot, an over-the-shoulder shot, and then everyone's respective close-up or single—Woody starts on a close-up of an actor and then, after that actor delivers the first line, he or she crosses the room and the camera moves with them, revealing the person they're talking to.

At that point, it's a medium two-shot.[3] After four or five lines of dialogue, though, he has the other actor drive toward the camera and the camera tracks back with them until it's a more typical master shot. Then you see the actors have changed places, the first one now standing in the background and the other one in the foreground, and the entire space is revealed. Then the actor in the background walks back into a nice over-the-shoulder, the two of them walk down the hallway, and it seamlessly melds into another two-shot.

I admired the way Woody used those moving masters because the scenes unfolded like a play. You are not manipulating the

2 Master shot: a wide shot encompassing the entire scene, keeping all the actors in view within the frame.

3 Two-shot: a shot encompassing two actors within the frame.

performance in the editing room; it's all right there. What I really like is that the actors' body language and movement, for example, when characters choose to walk toward or away from one another, can say even more about who the characters are than the dialogue they're speaking.

One of my favorite examples of where we applied this technique is a scene with Jennifer Aniston and Mike McGlone in their loft. She's pressing him to come clean about the reasons their marriage is in trouble; he hasn't shown any interest in having sex with her. As written, the scene is almost three pages long, and we shot it as one giant moving master where, in the end, he confesses that he's in love with somebody else. That was one of the first times I was able to do something like that, and at the end of the day, I felt a new kind of satisfaction. I felt I was now learning how to use the camera in my storytelling.

I like another scene where we used the moving master. It's with McGlone and John Mahoney on their back deck. It's simple. It's just a bunch of different framings, but it plays like a dance between the camera and the actors. I wanted to create a locked-in moment where they sit, talk, and move all in one shot. I have put those types of scenes in my movies ever since. For me, that's when I feel I'm a film-maker and not just a writer.

TRIAL AND ERROR

We cut the film in two different editing houses in Tribeca (both are gone now), and what I remember most is that the beginning of the movie wasn't working. There were a number of redundancies. As a young screenwriter, I used to be guilty of playing the same beat over and over in an effort to inform the audience, and this was painfully obvious when I saw the first pass.

And you always wonder, Why hadn't I caught the redundancies during thirty days of shooting. Why hadn't I seen it in the script?

It was on *She's the One* with my editor, Sue Graef, that I learned that the cutting of the film is actually your last rewrite of the script. A filmmaker learns how to tell a story on film in the editing room. We took a scene from the first ten minutes and moved it to around the thirty-minute mark, and we took a scene that came around that thirty-minute plot point and put it closer to the front. It was a simple flip-flop, but it worked—the scenes land nicely, as if they had been written that way.

The other thing that helped my writing moving forward was discovering what was needed for the scene to work and sometimes, more important, what wasn't needed. Cutting the heads and tails off scenes was a real eye-opener for me as well. Most times, the audience doesn't need to see the actor enter the room, turn on the lights, sit down on the chair, pick up the phone, and make the call. Usually, you can just cut to her on the phone. As the movie came together, it started to have a distinct rhythm. A good deal of that came from the script. I had written several scenes that I wanted to be linked together and play as one continuous conversation. We discovered in the edit that by cutting the tail off one scene and cutting the head off the scene that followed it, we could create a similar effect. As the scenes played off each other, the characters seemed to answer one another even though their scenes were disconnected. It not only helped with the pacing but it also created a few punch lines that weren't apparent in the screenplay.

Given the success of *McMullen*, I was given final cut, which meant that regardless of the notes the studio might give me, I had final say. Luckily for me, the studio loved the film and we got only one note. It was from Rothman. In the final scene of the movie, I walk down the dock with a cooler of beer to find my girl, Hope, standing in the boat with my father. In the original cut of this scene, for some unknown reason, I barely smile. Rothman said, "What's wrong with you? You have to smile when you see the girl at the end." Of course I did.

We did test screenings in Philadelphia, Washington, DC, and Los Angeles. I found it a valuable learning experience. I was able to sit with an audience and see in real time where the movie worked, where we got laughs, and where we didn't get laughs. Fortunately, those no-laugh moments were few.

The movie was playing well and the folks at Searchlight were happy. We all felt like we were going to have another hit on our hands.

TOM PETTY WANTS A MEETING

Up until that point, we had temp music in the various cuts, but it was time to add a permanent soundtrack. I thought we had to have *She's the One*, and I was about to write a letter to Springsteen, asking if we could use his song. Though I didn't expect him to give us the rights to his version, we were hoping to get the Wallflowers, a new band with a Springsteen-like hit called "6th Avenue Heartache," to cover the song.

Then, just as we began having internal conversations about approaching Bruce, I got a call from Robert Kraft, the president of Fox Music at the time, advising me to hold everything.

"Tom Petty has seen the movie and wants a meeting," he said.

"Jesus, yeah, of course." I was a huge Petty fan. "What's the deal?"

It turned out Petty was between albums, and this was a time when artists and bands were giving songs to movies for the tail credits. You could break a song there, like Sarah McLachlan did with "I Will Remember You."

"You have to fly back out to LA and meet with him."

"Sure," I said. "Just say when."

I flew out the next day. I rented a car and drove to the address I was given in the Pacific Palisades, a West LA neighborhood overlooking the Pacific. As I pulled up in front of his house, I had to remind myself of the bizarre turn my life had taken. I was still twenty-seven, and though I had shot *She's the One*, I was only a few years from being a production assistant at *Entertainment Tonight* and now I was about to meet Tom Petty.

"Come on in," he said, answering the door himself.

Tom was a nice guy who had genuinely liked my film and we made some small talk for a while. Then he wanted to get down to business.

"Ready to listen to the tune?"

"Absolutely," I said.

He walked me to his music room. I knew he had written a song for the movie and expected him to play me a tape or CD. But instead, he sat down on a chair and picked up a guitar. He plugged it into an amp, oblivious to me sitting there in shock that I was about to get a private Petty concert, and started to play the song "Walls." After strumming the last chord, he looked at me.

"It's a new song," he said. "What do you think?"

"Yeah," I said, blown away. "I love it."

"Do you want it for the movie?" he asked.

"Yeah. Definitely."

"I have another one," he said.

He played "Angel Dream."

"What'd you think of that one?" he asked.

I didn't know what to think other than it was also tremendous.

"Is that one better than the first?" he asked.

"I think they're both great," I said.

"I got one more," he said.

He played "Hung Up and Overdue." All three had a similar vibe, especially with him playing and singing solo two feet in front of me, and yet all were different, though each one easily related with what I was trying to get across in the movie.

"Which one do you think would work best?" he asked.

I immediately thought of *The Graduate*. I have always loved that film, and one of the elements that has made that movie resonate over the years, over generations really, is the way director Mike Nichols used Simon & Garfunkel's music across the entire film. Those classic songs were much more than the soundtrack. They became part of the narrative. I wondered if I could do something like that with Petty's songs.

"Would you ever be up for doing something like *The Graduate*?" I asked.

"What do you mean?" he said.

"Well, rather than one song, why don't we use all three? Maybe we use one as a theme and the others in different places. Maybe we assign one to each character or a situation. We could extract the melody from 'Walls [Circus]' and play it in different places. With three songs from you, the music begins to define a theme and a feeling."

"I like that idea," he said. "Let me think about it and talk to my manager."

Some two weeks after that meeting, I flew back to LA from New York and sat down with Petty, his producer, Rick Rubin, and the guys in Petty's band, the Heartbreakers. We talked about which songs I wanted to use, which they thought worked, and where they might go. The next day we were in the studio, with the film on a screen in front of them, and the band was playing live to spots in the film and writing brand-new music for other parts. It was going well and got even better when Tom said he had two songs that were left off his most recent album, *Wildflowers*.

"If we're doing three songs and we got these instrumental pieces, why not put in another song or two?"

The thing had evolved from a single song to three songs and a score. Then Tom added two more songs. And then while we were in the studio, Tom said that with five songs and other music, he might as well turn all this into an album. So not only does Tom Petty write a few tunes for the flick, end up doing the score, now he's going to release a new album with the Heartbreakers that would be called *She's the One*.

This was as good a start as you can have in Hollywood. I thought this was always how it was going to be.

SIX

NO LOOKING BACK

W ith *She's the One* in postproduction, I started to give thought to
   what I would write next.

I was happy with the tone of both *The Brothers McMullen* and
She's the One, but the films were very similar, and like so many young
artists, I didn't want to be pigeonholed. I felt that I had a broader
range in me.

There were three films that made up what I called my Texas
trilogy. *The Last Picture Show, Tender Mercies,* and *Hud* were three of
my favorite films and still are. All three films are quiet dramas with
understated performances. The filmmakers Peter Bogdanovich, Bruce
Beresford, and Martin Ritt embraced minimalist storytelling and
restraint with their camera work. They were telling honest stories
about regular folks in the real world, which was something I was
always attracted to as a viewer. And they were not looking for laughs.

That's what I wanted to do next. I wanted to hold a mirror up to the world I knew and reflect it back as honestly as I could.

As such, I began to write *Long Time, Nothing New*, the story of people my age in a small town, looking for a way out.

I wanted to keep it real. I wanted to look at the dreamers who couldn't articulate their dreams. They just knew there was more to life than what they were living. They had a burning desire to get out of their hometown but had no idea where to go or what to do. This wasn't going to be a movie about the ordinary working-class person who dreams of being a painter, a novelist, or a rock star and, halfway through the movie, pulls that old typewriter out of the closet, sits down, and writes the masterpiece. The people in my new story were stuck in a rut. Same shit, different day, or *Long Time, Nothing New*.

A big part of what I loved about my Texas trilogy was how important it was to each filmmaker to give the audience a sense of place, from the sleepy little town in *The Last Picture Show* to the roadside motel and gas station in *Tender Mercies*. These places weren't Anytown, USA. They felt specific and unique, though unlike any I encountered growing up on Long Island. Yet the characters and their desires, fears, and dreams were universal. Specific and universal. That was the key and that's what I was after.

Having grown up on the South Shore of Long Island, I spent my summers at the beach, primarily Long Beach. As vibrant and full of life as Long Beach was during the summer, it was equally quiet, still, and melancholy during the winter. Anyone who has been to a beach community during the off-season knows what I'm talking about. Long before I wrote one word of my new script, I knew that was going to be the setting for this screenplay.

At the time, I lived in a two-bedroom apartment on Horatio Street in Manhattan. It was a doorman building and cockroach-free.

I had turned the second bedroom into an office, the writing room I had always imagined. One night, I went out and bought Springsteen's *Tracks*, a four-album set of unreleased songs, B-sides, and demos. For Springsteen fans like me, this was an event—sixty-six songs from different parts of Bruce's career, all finished and remastered and accompanied by liner notes that explained where they fit into his body of work.

I sat up late into the night, listening, reading, and absorbing the music into the library of Bruce in my head. For obvious reasons the song "Iceman" got under my skin—more specifically the opening lines.

"Sleepy town ain't got the guts to budge/Baby, this emptiness has already been judged/I wanna go out tonight, I wanna find out what I got."

The song was an outtake from *Darkness on the Edge of Town* and I played it over and over. One line stuck in my head: "Sleepy town ain't got the guts to budge." By the twentieth time I listened, I was hearing it differently.

"Small-town girl ain't got the guts to budge."

That small-town girl became a character in *Long Time, Nothing New*. Her name was Claudia, and she was a waitress in the small town where she had always lived. "Small-town girl ain't got the guts to budge." The song let me feel the yearning and desperation inside that small-town girl whose eyes were cast a thousand miles from where she was.

In the early drafts of the script, I was going for more an ensemble story like *Picture Show*—some characters who had a way out, others who tried to find one, and others who knew they were anchored in that small town forever. But through various drafts, *Long Time, Nothing New* turned into a story about Claudia and the choice she had to make between two guys. One was an ex-boyfriend who re-turns to town intending to rekindle their relationship and take her the hell out of there. The other was his former best friend and now Claudia's fiancé, a regular Joe who will never leave town.

I felt like I was writing the hell out of the script because I knew these people. Not only were they modeled after friends, but I also threw a lot of myself in there, all the conflicts and emotions of my younger years, before that fateful day with my advisor at SUNY Albany.

By this time, Searchlight was testing a cut of *She's the One,* and audience reaction came back through the roof. Everyone was thrilled. Studio executives wanted to blow it out with a strong platform (or limited) release starting the same weekend *McMullen* had hit theaters a year earlier. Why mess with a formula that had grossed more than $10 million? Only this time, they expected to do double or triple that number.

Everything in the world was going my way. And that's when the walls came tumbling down.

YOUNG AND NOT KNOWING ANY BETTER

Buoyed by the good news of the tests and the success of *McMullen,* my agents decided to negotiate a Woody Allen–type deal for me with the studio. It was a "put" deal, which basically stipulated that Fox Searchlight would green-light any script I wanted to make, sight unseen, as long as the budget was under $15 million, starting with *Long Time, Nothing New.* I would make a movie for them every year or two.

In retrospect, it was a bold position to take for a kid whose first "real" movie was still a few months from being released. And as we sat at the agency's conference table, my gut told me as much. The folks at Fox have been good to me; why do we need to play hardball? However, my team assured me it was the right time to ask. Of the five movies Fox Searchlight released in their first year of business, *McMullen* was the big hit, and that, my agents said, gave me leverage.

There was a tense phone call with Tom Rothman ("What happened? Didn't we do good by you?" he asked), and an even more uncomfortable lunch with Fox Entertainment chairman and CEO Bill Mechanic, who met me at a corner table in the studio commissary.

Mechanic said, "Why would you ask for this? We thought you were part of this family."

I was devastated.

"Look, it's my team," I said. "I'm just listening to them, following their lead." What did I know? I'm not in the business two years at this point.

Despite a release date that had seemingly been set in stone only months earlier, Searchlight moved *She's the One* behind *Emma* and *Tin Cup* and reduced their support. The film was released on 459 screens on August 23, 1996, grossing $4,550 per theater for a weekend gross of $2.1 million. The next weekend, the screen count went up to 464, but the screen average fell off only 6 percent. Normally, with these kinds of numbers, this is when the studio takes the film wider, meaning they up the number of screens the film plays on. However, that wasn't the case. *She's the One* still went on to gross $9.5 million and was Searchlight's biggest hit that year, but the message was clear: I had blown it. Then the studio passed on *Long Time, Nothing New*.

My agents told me not to worry and promised they would find another buyer. They shopped the script without any bites. To make the deal more attractive, we slashed the proposed budget from $15 million to $12 million to $8 million and then to $6 million.

As my agents shopped for a deal, they suggested I branch out as an actor. Their argument was, if I wanted to continue making my own films, I should act in larger studio movies and thereby become more famous. If I were more famous, it would help get my films financed. It seemed to make sense except for the fact that I never considered myself an actor. I enjoyed acting in my own films, but I knew what went into those performances. I wrote toward what I thought were my strengths as an actor and I later massaged those performances in the editing room. In other words, I knew my limitations. Because of this, I had passed on a number of acting jobs that came my way after *McMullen* hit theaters. But with three films under my belt, I felt maybe now I was ready. I told my agents, "Let's go find something."

One of the first scripts they sent me was *Saving Private Ryan*. The D-Day epic followed a group of soldiers as they searched for the last surviving brother of four soldiers who marched into the deadly maw of battle on Omaha Beach. The script came with a note: This is Steven Spielberg's next project. My agent said I should look at the part of Sarge since I was too old, at age thirty, to play any of the privates. After reading the script, I knew playing Sarge required some heavy lifting and I knew I was not quite ready for that, or even capable of it, back then. But I thought I could take on another part, that of PFC Reiben, the wiseass from Brooklyn. He was a sarcastic pain in the ass.

"That I can do!" I told my agent. "Can you put me up for Reiben instead of Sarge?"

"Let me see what they say," he replied.

In the meantime, my agents found two companies willing to split the price tag for *Long Time, Nothing New*. Gramercy Pictures offered to put up $3 million, and an overseas fund called Silver Streak signed for the other half.

I was ecstatic. I quit thinking about whether *Private Ryan* was going to happen and concentrated on the good news. I was going to make my third movie.

SHUTTING THE MOVIE DOWN

Casting *Long Time, Nothing New* was a reality check. Instead of the long line of up-and-coming actresses vying for the lead in *She's the One*, I was greeted with a string of turndowns, starting with Patricia Arquette and Elisabeth Shue. Marisa Tomei was briefly interested, but she wanted Claudia changed from a waitress to a nurse, which would've required a complete rewrite since half the movie took place in a diner. Finally, my new manager, Rick Yorn, suggested his latest signee, Lauren Holly, who came in and nailed her audition. I had my lead.

Finding the right guy to play Lauren's fiancé was even harder. After seeing numerous actors, someone at PolyGram—the parent company of Gramercy—mentioned they were putting out a new Bon Jovi album and suggested casting him as Claudia's boyfriend.

Jon had held his own alongside Whoopi Goldberg, Gwyneth Paltrow, and Kathleen Turner in *Moonlight and Valentino*, and I knew Jon's New York acting coach, Harold Guskin. I called him up.

"What do you think?" I asked.

"This guy is fully committed to acting. This isn't just a hobby," Harold said. "He's the real deal. You should absolutely sit down with him."

We met for lunch in SoHo, and within ten minutes I was sold. He grew up in a working-class neighborhood in New Jersey, similar to my Long Island hometown, and he was a great guy. It was like we already knew each other. He knew he had the part before he left the room.

But the good vibes disappeared quickly. One afternoon, less than a week into preproduction, I was working with Lauren and Jon in an East Village rehearsal space, when we were interrupted with an urgent phone call. Excusing myself, I went into another room, where my agents told me to brace myself for bad news: The movie's co-investor, Silver Streak, did not have the money that they said they did.

"They don't have any money."

"Are you kidding me?" I said. "What does this mean?"

"You're probably going to have to shut down."

Stunned, I walked back into the room and said, "Why don't we cut rehearsal short today."

What do I do when the shit hits the fan? I call the old man. My dad met me at a bar downtown, where I told him I did not want to let the movie die. I had gone through too much to get it this far. Too much was at stake. Besides, how would this look if I couldn't get this film off the ground? We decided that was not an option. As my father had on *McMullen*, I decided I would put my own money into the film.

I took nearly every dollar I had made in the business up to that point and put it into the film. Though it was enough to keep us in preproduction, I knew I had to figure out another major move if I wanted to actually make the movie. Fortunately, Tom Rothman was there when we needed him again. Bart Walker, my agent, had somehow convinced the Fox studio executive to buy the international rights for around $2.5 million—enough to save the movie.

Once on the set, all the preproduction drama was forgotten. We shot for thirty-five days in Rockaway Beach, the perfect setting for my sleepy seaside town. With $5.5 million, we had enough dough that I was able to make everything look exactly the way I envisioned. I fell in love with production design and details. My DP, Frank Prinzi, and I drew from Edward Hopper paintings and one of the movies that inspired the screenplay, *Tender Mercies*. There are a few shots and sequences where you can see the influence. Creative work sometimes starts with imitation but finishes with inspiration.

At night, I raced back to the city to watch dailies and marveled at the look we captured. The movie was gorgeous. Only one problem cropped up during production, but it was a big one. Gramercy's executives wanted the title changed. Anything but *Long Time, Nothing New*, they said. They feared critics would write, "Long time in our seat. Nothing new from Ed Burns."

They threw a thousand titles at me until they came up with one they liked: *No Looking Back*. Did I like it? No. But the folks at the studio seemed to like the movie and were promising us a meaningful release. Their argument was a strong one: We want this movie to work as much as you do and we'll have a better chance at success if we change the title. As a result, I said I was okay with the title.

In retrospect, I wouldn't advise rolling over like that. Years later, long after the movie came out, I was in a video store in the West Village and came across *No Looking Back*. I knew the people at Gramercy who had insisted on retitling the picture hadn't thought about the movie since it left theaters. But I had. I still thought about it. I was thinking about it there in the video store: *No Looking Back*, a Film by Edward Burns. Yes, it was my film—but not my title.

No Looking Back in Rockaway Beach, Queens

LONG TIME, NOTHING NEW

As it turned out, my original title stayed in a part of the movie. Before it changed, Rick Yorn, my manager, introduced me to his younger brother, Pete Yorn, then an unsigned singer-songwriter. Pete's style and sound seemed like a good fit with the feeling I wanted to convey in the picture. He wrote and performed a song called "Long Time, Nothing New," and it stayed in the movie, playing over the tail credits. If you want to hear it, Pete released it years later on his *Back & Fourth* album.

Although it reminds me to this day that I still haven't made my film about a bunch of guys who are stuck in a rut in a small town (I will one day), it is also part of a pretty special soundtrack. I was able to use songs from Sheryl Crow, Glen Campbell, Lynyrd Skynyrd, the Allman Brothers, Bruce Springsteen, and Patti Scialfa, among others.

BRUCE

Meeting Bruce was one of those happy accidents. In the fall of 1996, he was about a year into his The Ghost of Tom Joad Tour. My brother and I, being Springsteen fanatics, drove to Wallingford, Connecticut, to see him at the Oakdale Theatre. I still remember the place and date, as most Bruce fans do with the shows they have seen, especially the great ones.

Using some connections, we found our way backstage to a room that seemed like the designated party room. There was a table full of food, a bar, and a couple dozen people with backstage passes pressed onto their clothes or dangling around their necks. We got a drink and stood around for about forty-five minutes before realizing Bruce was not part of this gathering, and it didn't feel like he was going to show up.

Unable to walk back out the front of the theater at that hour, we strolled through a long corridor that wound around the back of the theater. A roadie told us to look for the exit ramp and follow it to the parking lot. As we walked along, we saw Bruce and one of his buddies heading toward us. I elbowed my brother.

"Holy shit, it's Bruce," I said under my breath.

A step or two later, Bruce's friend, Matty Delia, looks at me and flashes a smile.

"Hey, man! You're that guy from the Irish brothers movie, right?"

"Yeah," I said.

"Bruce, it's the kid from that *McMullen* movie."

We all said hi, shook hands, and Bruce said, "You guys live up in Connecticut?"

"Nah," I said. "We drove up from Manhattan."

He looked at us with disbelief.

"It's five hours from Manhattan," he said.

"Yeah, but we're big fans," I said.

"In that case," he said, "we're having a drink. Right now."

We went back to his dressing room and spent the next two and a half hours talking, just me, my brother, Bruce, and his buddy. It turned out to be more fortuitous than I imagined. You can't imagine the thrill when a year later, Bruce visited the set of *No Looking Back* with his buddy Matty. We were shooting at a gas station in Old Tappan, New Jersey, that happened to be owned by a friend of

Matty's. We ended up casting Matty to play one of the car mechanics in the film.

And then, two years later, as I put together *No Looking Back*, I was able to use a few songs from Bruce's *Tunnel of Love* album and a few from Patti's excellent solo album, *Rumble Doll*. Instead of going to the studio's music department, I called Bruce directly and invited him and Patti to see the movie.

"If you like the way we used the songs, I'd love to talk about how we can make it work out," I said.

He came and really dug the movie, as I suspected he would. He was friendly with Bon Jovi, and his working-class sensibilities were aligned with the story about people stuck in this small seaside town. After the screening, he gave me a thumbs-up.

It's a blessing to find yourself working in this business. You get to do the thing you actually want to do and sometimes, in the process, you get to meet and work with your heroes. Regardless of what would later happen with this film, I had that.

SEVEN
SAVING PRIVATE RYAN

The final edits to *No Looking Back* were made in London. Why London? Because two days before Christmas, I got an early gift. I received word that I had been cast as PFC Reiben in Steven Spielberg's *Saving Private Ryan*. I had never met Spielberg. Nor did I audition. He had seen both *McMullen* and *She's the One* and word was he wanted an authentic New York kid. Talk about lucky.

Soon after the holidays, I picked up my phone and it was Tom Hanks. He was calling to welcome me to the production. He explained that before production started, a bunch of us, including himself, Tom Sizemore, Vin Diesel, Barry Pepper, Giovanni Ribisi, Adam Goldberg, Jeremy Davies, and I would enter a rigorous eight-day boot camp. Months later we found ourselves in the hands of the film's military advisor, Dale Dye, who put us through a rigorous training out in the field, with little sleep and food. Dye wanted us to feel stressed and fatigued, and we did. More important, he wanted us to feel like soldiers. He reminded us that we would be representing the men of his fraternity who died on the beach for our freedom, and that he was going to make sure we honored them by looking like real soldiers. He was going to drive us hard, but it was going to be worth it. And it was.

The day after boot camp ended, we met Spielberg for the show-and-tell. We all had our weapons, in my case the BAR (Browning Automatic Rifle), and were in wardrobe. The uniforms were so realistic that the boots were exact replicas of those worn by soldiers in the D-Day invasion, and made by the actual Minnesota manufacturer of the original boots. Some of the guys had met Spielberg before; this was my first time. Personable and matter-of-fact, he expressed his eagerness to get started, spoke a bit about his overall vision, and said, "See you tomorrow" for the first day of shooting.

I was in awe. Here I was, standing with two more heroes of mine the day before shooting what would go down as one of the greatest war films of all time.

My first scene was a long dolly shot of Tom Hanks, me, and the rest of the guys walking through the field soon after we'd taken on the mission to find Matt Damon. Steven was about fifty yards away across the field, looking through the camera. Needless to say, I was nervous, this being my first scene in a huge Hollywood movie. My first movie, McMullen, cost $25,000. Total. The lens on Steven's camera was probably triple that figure. I had four or five lines of dialogue. I was pretty together until I heard Steven yell, "Action." Then all of a sudden, I was overcome by fear—or by the reality of the moment, the enormity of it. This was the first time I had spoken a line of dialogue that I didn't write, and I was doing it with Tom Hanks and Steven Spielberg on the set of a movie that was epic in size, cost, and ambition.

It was up to me to start the scene, to deliver lines, but as I said them—or tried to—I could hear my voice crack and see my hands shaking. A moment later, Spielberg called, "Cut."

Hanks leaned in close to me and said, "First-inning jitters. That's all right. Just calm down, man. It's going to be okay."

We did another take and I was no better the second time through. Again, Tom pulled me aside.

"What's going on, man? You've got to settle down. You can do this."

Steven called "action" a third time and while this take was a little better, it was far from good. Again, Tom whispered in my ear, "Dude, what the hell is going on? I've seen your flicks, I know you can act, and this isn't acting."

So much for the authentic New York kid. I was convinced I would be taken aside at lunch and told my character was going to be killed off the next day. Fortunately, I got my shit together on the next take, and three months later, I was standing on the bridge with Damon in the final scene of the film. However, it should be noted that this first scene with Hanks did not make it into the final cut of the flick.

Most directors would have stepped in after my first botched take, offered some notes, and inadvertently rattled my confidence. But that wasn't Steven's approach with us. He allowed us several takes to figure things out for ourselves. So much so that he didn't provide any direction for almost two weeks. We did our scenes in two or three takes and then moved on. No feedback. Nothing. The cast figured he hated what we were doing and speculated which one of us would be fired first.

Finally, as week three got under way, Steven had us repeat a scene four or five times. After the fifth take, something more surprising

Taken moments before my first scene in *Saving Private Ryan*

happened. He gave us direction. Then we got a little more direction. Finally, after the eighth or ninth take, Steven was satisfied and we broke for lunch.

Among Adam Goldberg, Vin Diesel, and I, we had a few guys who had written or directed indie films, and we regularly tried to pick Steven's brain. This time, we were curious about why, after a couple of weeks of silence, he gave us direction.

"Because today you didn't know what the hell you were doing," he replied, as if it were obvious.

He went on to say that he had cast all of us for specific reasons. In his mind, we were very much like the characters we were playing and he wanted to bring as much of that to the screen in as natural a manner as possible. To that end, he said, "I like to give my actors three takes to figure it out. If I step in after the first take and give you a note, especially with young actors, you'll hear me rather than your own voice.

"That might rattle you, too. Hurt your confidence. Or cause you to question your choices. And who even gets it right on the first or second take?

"So I'll give you time to find it," he continued. "Especially in an ensemble piece where you have four or five guys acting together. It's going to take everyone a little time to find the beats and gel."

"When do you decide to step in?" I asked.

"If I feel like you're going in the wrong direction," he said. "And then, only with a little note, as little as possible. I'd rather you guys find it."

From that day forward, I changed my approach with actors. I, too, now give the time and room to figure it out. I'm sure I was guilty on a few occasions of stepping in too early and giving an actor a note. Like a lot of young filmmakers, I thought being a director meant you were always giving direction. This is not the case. It's about knowing *when* to give direction.

ON THE JOB

The entire experience of shooting *Saving Private Ryan* was a life changer. Both Steven and Tom became not only good friends but also mentors. When my family came to visit the set that summer, I introduced Steven to my father and uncle. Both were vets, both were big-time cops, and both were natural storytellers who had an endless stream of colorful tales about the streets of New York in the sixties and seventies that captivated Steven. I mentioned to him that I had been thinking about turning their stories and others like them into a movie, an Irish American multigenerational saga set against the police department in the 1970s. I imagined it as my *Godfather*. Steven thought it was a great idea and after *Saving Private Ryan* wrapped, he gave me a deal with his studio, DreamWorks, to write the script, which I was calling *On the Job*.

I wrote obsessively in my new apartment on 11th Street off the West Side Highway. My work consumed me. I was writing my dream script for Spielberg's company. However, this business is all about highs and lows, peaks and valleys.

On March 27, 1998, I woke up to the first review of *No Looking Back* in my fax machine and it was not good. Nor were those that followed. Other than Stephen Holden of *The New York Times*, who offered criticisms but got my overall intention, it was one bad review after another. They hurt. I was used to praise. *McMullen* and *She's the One* had spoiled me.

After the opening day took in a meager $44,000 against the $6 million budget, the studio shelved its plans to release the movie to more theaters. I would painfully refer to the picture as *No One Saw It*.

However, here's the thing about movies that seem to disappear without a trace. With hundreds of cable channels and Netflix and iTunes, these movies live on forever. Years later, I was working with Dustin Hoffman in a movie called *Confidence*, and he mentioned he just caught some movie of mine on late-night cable. He said it was terrific and he loved the acting, but he didn't know the name of it. He said, "It's the one where you're with the girl in the seaside town." Highs and lows.

GIVING LA A SHOT

Around the time my movie was bombing, I began doing long-lead press for *Saving Private Ryan*, and that provided a winning distraction. The movie's ad campaign was massive, all-consuming. By the opening weekend in July, Steven Spielberg's World War II masterpiece was at the center of every conversation about movies, and the reviews proved the buzz was deserved. "A watershed picture," said one paper. Another praised its "dazzling virtuosity." The *San Francisco Chronicle* aptly said, "An overwhelming experience."

It was for me. Suddenly, I was at the Deauville Film Festival in France, sitting next to Steven, Tom Hanks, and Tom Sizemore for the black-tie premiere. Afterward, there was a standing ovation. Then it was off to the Oscars. I didn't attend the Academy Awards, where Steven took the Best Director honors and the film captured a total of five statues. I did attend all the parties and experienced a part of the business that I'd only dreamed about when I was banging away on all those scripts after college. And that wasn't so long ago.

In early 1999, I decided it was time to take up permanent residency in sunny California. I moved to LA and opened a production office on the outskirts of West Hollywood. I had my deal with Dream-Works for *On the Job*, and I was being offered starring roles in movies. I was in a good place.

For the first time in my screenwriting career, I was taking my time writing the script. I promised myself I would not rush the process. There was no deadline and this script had to be great. Unlike my three previous films, for which I could draw upon my own experiences, the script for *On the Job* required extensive research. I had several sit-downs with my father, interviewing him about his first days on the job in East Harlem, 1966, on through his time working at police headquarters in the 1980s. I also devoured every book, fiction and nonfiction, I could get my hands on that dealt with the NYPD during that time. I combed through back issues of *Spring 3100*, the cop magazine for the NYPD that my uncle Pat had given me. Only after getting a handle on who the cops were at that time, and what the job felt like back then, did I sit down to outline my story.

I wanted to write an epic. An Irish American *Godfather* that revolved around the cops instead of the mob. In the way *The Godfather* can be looked at as a family saga dressed up as a gangster movie, I wanted to tell my family story dressed up as a cop film. The film was centered around a young cop, Tommy Reilly, who would be played by me, as he leaves the police academy in the mid-1960s, and follows him through the first decade of his career. A year and a half after starting, I finally finished *On the Job* and submitted it to Steven and the executives at DreamWorks.

My producing partner, Michael Nozik, whom I had been working with since we met at Sundance, budgeted the film at $25 million. Given that number, we knew we needed to attract a major movie star to play the patriarch of the Reilly clan, the chief of detectives, Dan Reilly.

We put together our wish list of movie stars and began the process of making offers. This would be my first experience trying to attach an eight-hundred-pound gorilla to one of my movies. What I soon discovered was that it takes these guys a long time to read scripts and make decisions. Avoid it at all costs if you can. Waiting six months for a movie star to read your script can suck the life out of you and kill the momentum of your fledging production.

And that's what happened to us. After six months, we still hadn't gotten a response from our first choice (who will remain nameless).

It was now January 2000 and I hadn't directed a movie since the spring of 1997. I was antsy to get back behind the camera. I read about other filmmakers who will spend years trying to get a movie made. Personally, I just don't have that patience. No one movie is so important that I would be willing to go years without being behind the camera. It's just too much fun making a movie, and I got into this business because I have a lot of stories to tell and, fortunately for me, a lot of little stories, and little stories don't need movie stars.

I had a two-part plan. First, while we waited for our movie star to read *On the Job*, I dusted off the script I was writing on the set of *Saving Private Ryan* and started rewriting. Second, I needed to find another acting job.

Rick, my manager, was set on finding a movie as good as *Saving Private Ryan*. He repeatedly said, "We can't make a wrong move." He paraphrased Warren Beatty: You don't need to make three movies a year. Just make sure the next one is a great one. But it was impossible to find one that we felt was great. How many *Private Ryan*s come along each year? Or every five years? Besides, as much as I loved my *Ryan* experience, I didn't think of myself as an actor. I was a writer/director and I was busy writing my epic. So it was easy to pass on some of the things that came my way.

I passed on *Practical Magic*, the comedy with Sandra Bullock and Nicole Kidman. Then, despite a big offer, I passed on the science fiction picture *The Deep Blue Sea*. And I bailed at the eleventh hour on *Frequency*, director Gregory Hoblit's film about a firefighter father and his police detective son who reconnect years after the father has died. Interestingly enough, the more you pass, the more you find yourself doing nothing but second-guessing yourself, and that's how it was with me until we found *15 Minutes*.

It was the story of a New York City firefighter and a detective who team up to stop some Eastern European thugs on a murder spree. The project seemed to have all the elements we wanted, starting with a script from writer-director John Herzfeld, who was coming off an award-winning experience in his previous film, *Don King: Only in America*. I was the co-lead, with none other than Robert De Niro. One of my criteria when looking at acting jobs was, I wanted to work with people I could learn from. And who better to go to acting school with than De Niro? On paper, this was just what we were looking for. The perfect follow-up to *Ryan*.

During the course of making that film, two things happened. One is that I was back on a movie set for the first time since making *Ryan*. It had been a couple of years. And I realized how much I missed it. The second thing is that after shooting the first half of the movie in Los Angeles, the production moved to New York for the second half, and while there, I said to myself, "Okay, I need to get back home." I remember exactly where I was. We were shooting a scene in Battery Park. My character was sitting in a cab before he has a confrontation with Kelsey Grammer's character. As I waited in the back of the cab for John to call "action," I asked myself what I was doing living in LA.

I missed New York, my hometown, my muse. And as much as I loved getting to work with Bobby D, I missed being a filmmaker. I promised myself that as soon as *15 Minutes* wrapped, I would move back home and make a movie.

Between shots on the set of *15 Minutes* with Robert De Niro

arlier, after I had set up my production office in Los Angeles, I needed someone to help me run my company, which is how I met Aaron Lubin, my now longtime producing partner. Recommended by my agent, Aaron came in for an interview. After graduating from law school, he joined an agency where he started as an assistant, then moved into development at a studio-based production company, and was now looking to produce on his own.

We clicked the moment we began talking about movies. Like me, Aaron turned out to be a die-hard Woody Allen fan. But I was looking for more than someone who had tastes similar to mine. At the time, *On the Job* was my number one priority and, as I explained, I wanted someone who would complement and challenge me. Aaron was that guy.

Before leaving for Europe to start *Ryan*, I had begun work on an outline for the movie that would eventually be titled *Sidewalks of New York*. It was about a group of interconnected young New Yorkers moving in and out of relationships. I took the outline with me to London, and during my downtime on the set, I started to write the script. I drew from people I knew back in New York and from stories the guys and I on *Ryan* shared about our relationships. How do you pass the time in a foxhole? Like real soldiers, we talked about girls.

I came up with the idea of shooting it documentary style, while sitting in that foxhole, watching the way Steven was making *Saving Private Ryan*.

I had made three movies of my own and knew both the difficulty and the importance of making a schedule and adhering to it. Steven flew through the scenes. *Ryan* was scheduled to shoot for sixty-six days and we wrapped in fifty-nine. That does not happen. Ever. Movies go over schedule. Big movies like *Ryan* go way over schedule. *Saving Private Ryan* was the polar opposite of a small indie. Steven had re-created a French village on another continent; he had remade Normandy on a beach in County Wexford, Ireland; and then he had restaged the invasion with two thousand extras—and came in under schedule! I was beyond impressed.

I think a primary reason we were able to shoot so quickly was the style in which we were shooting. The film was shot with a lot of handheld camera work and available light. He was going for the grainy feel of period documentary footage, the kind the army itself took. Therefore, there was not a lot of downtime between shots and setups. No big lights to move. Just reposition the camera operator and call "action" again.

As I watched him employ this technique, I thought, "Wait a second. I make low-budget indie films. Why don't I shoot an entire film like this?" Consequently, as I continued to write the script for *Sidewalks of New York*, I envisioned it shot in this documentary style.

And so while in our holding pattern with *On the Job*, I had Aaron read that first draft of *Sidewalks of New York*. I explained that I wanted to make the film this year and that meant a low budget, a run-and-gun sensibility, and a short shooting schedule. More important, I did not want to get locked into the slog of chasing a movie star and trying to raise a ton of money.

"So what are you thinking?" he asked.

"We do this movie for a million dollars," I explained.

As I saw it, the lower the budget, the more control I would have. The more control I had, the more freedom I would have to make the movie I envisioned. Ultimately, I believed this would result in a better movie and moviemaking experience.

Sidewalks started as a loose idea about the excitement of being single in New York. I was fascinated by the idea that you could go out on any night, walk into a bar, not know anyone, and find yourself in bed with a stranger a few hours later. The next weekend, the girl or guy you hooked up with might do it again with someone new. I thought about how those parties are connected. You're not only connected to the person you slept with, but you are also connected to the people they are sleeping with. That was the jumping-off point.

All my friends at the time were single, and everyone had great stories of "Oh God, yeah, that night I did this or hooked up with that guy . . ." For someone like me who wrote small, talky romances, this was a landscape ripe with awkwardly funny and not so funny situations.

Both Aaron and my brother had read the script and thought it was funny, as did I when writing it, but when I picked it up again and reread it, I could see its problems. The structure still worked: six characters whose individual problems lead them in and out of bed with each other, showing everyone's interconnectedness. There was my character, a TV producer, who meets a teacher (Rosario Dawson) in a video store. Her ex-husband is a musician (David Krumholtz) who falls for a coffee shop waitress (Brittany Murphy). She's having an affair with her dentist (Stanley Tucci), whose Realtor wife (Heather Graham) is showing apartments to my TV producer.

But I saw that certain scenes needed to be trimmed or cut altogether, and new information added, so we would know more about certain characters.

In my rewrite, I cut all the expositional and setup scenes. I probably wouldn't have been able to do that without the passage of time. But now, a few years after having written the script, I no longer had an immediate emotional connection to scenes; I had forgotten how much time I spent writing them. As writers will attest, it's hard to delete a scene when you can still feel the pain of having said no to dinner invitations and weekend softball games.

It was a valuable lesson for me as a writer. I didn't have to explain everything to the audience. They didn't need twenty minutes of setup. I could trust they would get all the necessary information if they hung with the movie. The script was cut down to include only the pulp.

Once I decided to embrace the pseudodocumentary style, I looked to Woody Allen's *Husbands and Wives* to try and figure out what the rules of the universe were with this type of storytelling. More specifically, who were the camera crew and why were they filming these people? Where were they allowed to go? How would we use the testimonial-type interviews (now an essential part of reality TV and sitcoms like *The Office* and *Modern Family*)? Would the interviews take place before the camera crews were allowed into their lives? Would they take place a month after the crews had packed up and gone home? I decided that the crew sat down with our subjects once before and once after they were welcomed into the subjects' lives. There would also be spur-of-the-moment interviews that would take place right after an incident. These interviews were a valuable tool in setting up the story and establishing the characters, but it also proved helpful by filling in some story points and adding laughs. Now with the script done, it was time to find a cast.

Heather Graham was all set to play the Realtor, but the other four leads were up in the air. Casting director Laura Rosenthal recommended Brittany Murphy for the coffee shop waitress and Rosario Dawson as the newly divorced teacher. Though neither actress was widely known yet, you could tell on set that both would be big stars sooner rather than later.

I have to say I got very lucky with the cast. It's one thing when you're locking people up for two to three months and paying top dollar, and it's another deal when you're offering scale and a couple days work. But the fact that it was only a couple days worked in my favor. Stanley Tucci is a perfect example. One of my favorite actors ever since I saw him in Greg Mottola's first film, *The Daytrippers* (a great New York indie from the nineties), he lived in New York, and I thought if he was home and available, I might have a chance.

I saw him in the role of the philandering dentist and said, "We're going to need you for five days tops and you get to stay in New York." He barely paused before saying, "I'd love to." David Krumholtz was the same. I thought he was fantastic in *Slums of Beverly Hills* and I wanted him for the musician part. A day later, we had him. By the way, we still hadn't heard from our movie star for *On the Job*.

After getting our top choices for the leads in a matter of days, we debated nearly as long about who would be good to play my boss. I was brainstorming with Aaron and Laura in our production office on Broadway in SoHo, trying to think of a great New York actor we could cast in the part. I said, "We need somebody from New York." The movie was about New York.

I was excited that the actors we had cast looked like people I saw on the street every day, and I was equally excited about having returned to the city. I was home and back in my element, shooting run-and-gun and on the streets. Aaron had recently watched Tarantino's *Jackie Brown* and suggested Robert Forster.

"I think he's from Chicago," I replied, adding a moment later, "but what about Dennis Farina?"

Aaron reminded me that Dennis was from Chicago, too. However, the difference was that I knew Dennis and loved him.

He and I had met on *Saving Private Ryan*. He was an ex-cop who fell into acting, and I knew about cops. We hit it off immediately. I called him up and said, "Hey, I got this funny part. I don't know if you'd be into it, but—"

Before I finished, he said, "Absolutely, tell me when you want me."

Now that we had our cast, we had to go find the money. My goal was to make this movie for $1 million, while still shooting with a union crew in New York City. I was introduced to Margot Bridger (now a lifelong friend who has produced multiple movies with me), a protégé of Michael Nozik. I presented my plan to her. Margot had a true, no-frills indie spirit and knew how to make a small budget go a long way.

She agreed that we could make the film for that price, so we targeted a budget of $1 million and together we adopted an approach to make it happen. First, we had to make the movie in seventeen days. Second, because of our pseudodoc approach, we were able to cut a

Shooting *Sidewalks of New York* with Brittany Murphy and David Krumholtz

favorable deal with the unions where we consolidated crew positions. This also meant less transportation, less gear, and a generally smaller machine, which allowed us to move faster and grab the types of documentary style shots that are difficult to do when you have a full-scale feature film operation.

We didn't have an art department, so we identified existing locations that worked for our world. Instead of limiting us, this liberated the filmmaking. We were constantly grabbing interview segments or writing and shooting a new scene because all we really needed was a camera, which was always ready. We were unburdened by the typical waits for the respective departments to get a set ready.

Additionally, we had put together that terrific group of actors, all willing to work for scale, but we made a point to schedule their scenes so no actor worked more than four days, and they were almost all consecutive. Dennis Farina ended up doing all of his six scenes in one day.

Cathy Schulman, who would come on to produce the film, was on my management team at Artists Management Group. With her help, we found a foreign sales agent who was quickly able to get the entire film financed by selling to multiple territories. How does that work? Essentially, a sales agent sells the film's distribution rights, based on the cast and the script, to territories throughout the world. A good sales agent has relationships with the various local distributors within each country and can make these sales before the film gets made.

That meant we controlled the making of the picture and had the future domestic sale (and some remaining territories) as the financial upside. In other words, whatever we sold the film for in North America would be pure profit, to be divided up by the profit participants, which included me as well as the actors and crew members.

Plus, it meant we didn't have a financier or studio looking over our shoulder as we made the movie.

Sometimes movie sets are charmed environments where cast and crew all get along and you start to feel like a family. *Sidewalks* had that vibe almost from day one. An example of this is how we ended up shooting an improvised scene between Dennis and Rosario, who had stopped by to visit the set that day. An actor coming by set to hang out on their day off speaks to how much fun everyone was having on the movie. We were shooting inside a hotel that day. At lunch, I thought, why waste this convergence of talent? The three of us fleshed out an idea and as soon as we finished the scheduled scene, where I move into Dennis's apartment, we shot Rosario and Dennis having a moment in the hallway.

It was an example of the serendipitous goodness that came from having faith in my actors and allowing them to stretch and explore the work. This was the first film I had directed since working with Steven Spielberg, and I was applying his "hands off the actors" approach. I was giving them the three takes to find it on their own before I stepped in to offer notes, and very rarely did I need to. I also started to let some of the actors improvise. We would do three takes as scripted and then I would do a few more takes where I let the actors play. Sometimes it went nowhere, but in a few instances we got some great stuff, especially some of the scenes between Stanley and Heather. That was new to me, and it happened a lot on *Sidewalks*. It was indicative of the energy we all poured into that film. Not only did everyone get along, but they also became fast friends and shared a lot of laughs.

Shooting documentary-style freed me in the way that I had hoped. I could shoot a scene as scripted and then say, "All right, let's run across the street and do an interview. Then let's hustle down the street to the park and shoot another quick scene or improvise a new one. We shot in Central Park, Washington Square Park, and Tompkins Square Park, free locations that really sold the city, but there were other scripted locations like bars, restaurants, video stores, and diners that we couldn't afford. Given our $1 million limit, we simply didn't have it in the budget to own these locations and shut them down for our shoot.

So we developed a compromise, which we still use today. We pay a smaller fee, take a section of the location while the establishment stays open for business, and we shoot our scene. The studio film-maker and probably most indie filmmakers would tell you it can't be done. It will be too noisy because you can't control the sound, and you can't control the background extras, or the light. But we didn't have a choice. Maybe the sound wouldn't be perfect, but it sure would look great if we shot there. Besides, as a sound mixer friend of mine once said, "The sad reality of my job is that no one has ever walked out of a movie and said, 'Damn, that movie sounded terrific.'" When you're working with low budgets, you have to pick your battles.

We used this technique when shooting at Katz's Delicatessen on the Lower East Side. They agreed to let us shoot at a center table while they were open for business. No one ever complained that the scene in Katz's sounded too busy. We learned here that a great way of keeping a prized location is to make it easy for the owner to stay open, while we work with the constraints of our budget. We've used this technique on all of our later microbudget films.

When looking for an editor to cut the film, I knew I wanted to hire someone who worked primarily in documentaries. Frank Prinzi recommended a friend of his, David Greenwald. It was a fortuitous hire because after day one of shooting, David helped Frank and me approach our shooting style in a new way. David showed me a first cut of a scene where David Krumholtz meets Rosario after she's left the doctor's office with news that she is pregnant.

It was a textbook cut, exactly as I had shot it: There was the master, then the medium shots, then over-the-shoulders, and then close-ups.

Cuing up his screen again, he said, "I want to show you a different version of the same scene."

In this second version, he took the medium shot and, using jump cuts,[4] was able to splice together four different takes of the same handheld medium shot. It was fantastic. I was blown away by the look, the pace, and the way the jump cuts enabled us to land a joke in a different way. It also freed me up from having to worry about any continuity between takes. As I've explained before, I'd rather not worry about what arm Rosario was holding her handbag on. I watched intently as he played it again.

David then explained, "If you were shooting a doc, you'd only have the one angle. So you jump-cut in and out of the one shot to lose the information the audience doesn't need to know." It was another example of how sometimes your movie can dictate to you what it wants to be.

Years later, when I worked with writer-director Nick Willing, he put it like this: "When you're in the editing room, you need to listen to your film and not scream at your film." Meaning sometimes the movie you made is different from the movie you thought you were making.

After that first day, we stopped shooting traditional coverage and

---

4 Jump cut: an editing method in which you use the same basic camera angle in two shots, with the cut/edit being a jump in time.

approached each scene as if we were a documentary crew, that is, shooting most scenes from one handheld camera angle. This enabled us to shoot lean and work quick, and when you're trying to make a film in seventeen days, you need to do both.

It was a great experience, and we came in on schedule and on budget, but the best part of the process was that *Sidewalks* made me a filmmaker again.

And no, we still had not heard from the movie star who was reading *On the Job*. Nor would we.

AN INCREDIBLE SCREENING

Now that our film was in the can, we needed to find a distributor. We held a screening in July 2000 at the Harmony Gold Theater on Sunset Boulevard. The lights went down and the first set of interviews played. Each character was asked about the first time they'd had sex. Their answers, as well as the way they answered, were supposed to reveal details and aspects of their character that weren't scripted. Most of all, they were supposed to be engaging and funny. Take the answer my character gave about losing his virginity in a Cadillac.

TOMMY

(Being interviewed)

She pulled into the parking lot in her dad's new Cadillac. We got to talkin', and next thing I know . . . We're in the backseat kinda

goin' at it, so . . . It was pretty cool 'cause I had
never been in a Cadillac before.

I had thought that line might get a light chuckle; instead, it got
a laugh, a big laugh, a genuine laugh. I could see everyone got the
tone and dug the humor, and within five or ten minutes, I knew the
laughs were going to continue, and they did. At the thirty-minute
mark, in what we thought was the funniest scene in the film, Dennis
Farina's character sits in a hot tub while my character, Tommy,
primps in front of the mirror before going on his first date since
getting dumped by his girlfriend. Dennis advises me to put cologne
on my balls.

TOMMY

I won't put cologne on my balls.
You think I'm some sort of savage?

CARPO

I want you to listen to me on this.
I can smell your armpits from here, okay?
What do your balls smell like
when she sticks her face down there?
Just give those bad boys a spritz,
and she'll love it.

The scene brought the house down and both Aaron and I could
feel the theater crackle with energy. I turned to my producing partner
and said, "We're selling this movie tonight." When your movie plays
well, people stick around, and everyone lingered, wanting to discuss
the film. It felt great. We sold the movie later that week to Paramount

Classics for a price that easily made everyone their money back, and then some.[5] My old friend from Fox Searchlight's marketing department, David Dinerstein, was now running Paramount Classics. David and his team decided to wait twelve months before releasing the movie. They saw it as a fall picture and we were too late to release that fall. In the interim, they cut trailers, made posters, and entered the film in various festivals. In April 2001, *Sidewalks* opened the Los Angeles Film Festival, and five months later, I flew to Toronto for the Toronto International Film Festival, my first time taking part in that two-week celebration of movies.

The film screened at TIFF on Friday, September 7, and it felt like we had a hit.

9/11

The movie was scheduled to open on the following Friday, September 14. But then, on Tuesday the eleventh, the world as we knew it changed when al-Qaeda terrorists crashed two commercial jetliners into the North and South Towers of New York's World Trade Center, a third plane into the Pentagon, and a fourth, intended for the White House, into a field near Shanksville, Pennsylvania.

---

5   Since we sold *Sidewalks* for a nice seven-figure "advance" (an amount of money the studio pays in advance for the distribution rights before the movie has been released), the hope for further compensation is based on the success of the film. The studio must first get reimbursed for its advance as well as its costs marketing the film (which can be considerable) and its distribution fee (often around 25–30 percent of all revenue), and sometimes other costs, including interest and overhead. Once all of those costs are reimbursed, the film then gets in the black, and the producer will see net profit. Given this structure, it's unusual for a filmmaker to realize net profits.

I had returned home to New York City from Toronto, intending to do a week's worth of press leading into the opening of *Sidewalks*. On the tenth, after watching the Monday night football game with a friend, I went to the apartment of my then girlfriend and now wife, Christy Turlington, in the Village. The next morning, I overslept and scrambled to get downtown for a nine A.M. interview at a restaurant on Hudson and North Moore Streets.

I ran to the subway at 14th Street and jumped on the first train. To get to my place in Tribeca, I had to take a local. But because I wasn't paying attention, I got on an express. Instead of getting off at Franklin Street, I traveled another six blocks south to Chambers Street, got off, and decided to walk from there.

I encountered unusual congestion near the top of the staircase out of the station. As I pushed my way through the crowd, I saw why. Directly up ahead was the World Trade Center, and unbelievably, there was a hole in the North Tower—a large, ominous hole oozing black smoke. The first plane had probably hit three or four minutes earlier. People around me were speculating what had happened. One person said it was a small plane. Another said it was a bomb.

I immediately decided to run home and call Christy and my brother, both of whom lived in the Village. I turned around, took off, and nearly ran straight into actor Michael Imperioli. We had never met, but we recognized each other and traded looks that said, "What the fuck is going on?" Then we went our separate ways.

At my apartment, I grabbed my video camera, turned on the news, and began filming out the window. I called Christy but got her machine. I left a message, telling her that the tower had been hit. While I was on the phone with my brother, who was also watching the news, the anchorman said no one had confirmed any of the initial reports, whether it was a bomb, a plane, or an attack. Just as he said it might have been an accident involving a commercial airliner, I heard him say, "Oh my God, no! NO! Here comes another one."

With my camera pointed toward the towers, a second plane came from the south. I didn't see it hit, but I heard the impact and I could see on my viewfinder an enormous fireball explode from both sides of the building. A second later, I felt my windows shake from the blast. Then, as everyone knows, the rest of the day was profoundly sad and chaotic.

I was standing on the roof of my apartment building shortly after the second tower fell, watching that huge cloud of smoke, dust, debris, and death engulf Lower Manhattan. The cloud stopped five blocks south of my place. At one point, I walked over to the West Side Highway, where I saw all the firemen who'd been at the tower when it collapsed. Covered in dust, they stood drinking water, dazed, in shock, and emotionally devastated.

Later, my future brother-in-law walked down from Christy's apartment to check on me. The phone lines were down and they wanted to know if I was okay. After he found me, we walked together up to the Village. I remember passing by St. Vincent's Hospital on 12th Street. We saw doctors and nurses poised out front with stretchers and wheelchairs, but they didn't have anything to do. Not a single ambulance pulled up. It was absolutely still. It was one of the eeriest sights of the day.

Needless to say, a few days later, the movie's release was put on hold. The executives at Paramount Classics didn't feel they could release a movie called *Sidewalks of New York* that included numerous images of the World Trade Center, a few days after the tragedy.

The events that day turned the movie into a period piece. From that day forward, there would be movies that showed New York pre-9/11 and movies that were shot after. Our poster was a perfect example. The original was a mosaic of people's faces and NYC landmarks, including the Twin Towers.

The *Sidewalks of New York* premiere

NINE

ASH WEDNESDAY

When *Sidewalks* did come out a few months later, critics treated it with fondness. *The New York Times* said, "The time is right for a breezy, captivating New York romantic comedy." The film made nearly $3 million, the most of any release from Paramount Classics that year, and played across the country through the holidays. It ranks as my personal favorite because it most resembles the film I imagined in my head when writing the script. However, the best praise came about ten years later when David Krumholtz called to read me a letter he had just received with a new script. It said something to the effect of "Hi, David, I've been a fan of yours since seeing you in *Sidewalks of New York*. I'd like to meet with you to discuss my new movie. I hope you like it. Let me know if you're interested."

The letter was signed *Woody Allen*.

For me, I always wanted to be a storyteller like my heroes Woody,

William Kennedy, and Bruce Springsteen, whose bodies of work are clearly identifiable. As Howard Hawks said of his favorite directors, "I liked almost anybody that made you realize who in the devil was making the picture."

That said, for my fifth film, I wanted to try something different. I wanted to tell a more muscular story. I didn't have it in me to try and write another comedy, and certainly not another romance. There was and still is another genre that I've long been obsessed with: the gangster movie. In particular, I had recently been thinking about doing an Irish American gangster story. I had researched everything: the five point gangs that Scorsese explored in *Gangs of New York*, the Prohibition-era gangsters like Jack "Legs" Diamond, and New York's famous West Side gangsters like Owney Madden, Mickey Spillane, and the Westies.

I also thought that Catholicism should play a big part in whatever gangster story I was going to tell. I had always been fascinated when I read about how some of these cold-blooded killers made sure they went to Mass every Sunday. These guys were constantly looking for penance and I knew there was a movie script in that idea. I had just turned thirty and recently started going back to Mass myself. It was there in the pew one Sunday when I thought of playing with the idea of redemption in Hell's Kitchen. I would set this little crime drama against a religious holiday, Ash Wednesday, which became the title of the movie I eventually wrote.

I knew that if I tried to make a period film, I'd run into a lot of the same problems I encountered with *On the Job*, which by the way, at this point, was officially dead and stuffed into the drawer of my desk. The problem was that I couldn't find a contemporary reference to build my story around. So instead, I settled on the 1980s. I knew there was enough, architecturally, in different neighborhoods of Manhattan to convincingly sell that decade at a reasonable budget.

This story would be a departure for me in tone and genre. But as a writer, you can't hide from what moves you and what has shaped you. It's like mining. You keep digging and digging, hoping you'll find it, and what keeps you writing is that hope. For me, my family, my childhood, my neighborhood, my parish, and my ancestry all shaped me. They are the reasons I write what I write. So it was no surprise to me when I chose to revolve my story around another set of Irish Catholic brothers.

Ash Wednesday is the story of the Sullivan brothers, one of whom left town after running afoul of the Irish American mob. Three years later, he returns to check up on his wife, putting everyone's lives in danger.

I was off to a good start when I wrote the opening scene, a flashback where the younger of the two brothers hears some gangsters talking about how they're going to whack his older brother that night. When they go to the head to take a leak, he follows them and kills the three men. He then confesses his sins to the neighborhood priest, who helps him get the hell out of Dodge, but under the condition that he never come back.

And yet, three years later our man returns.

Financing came through a good friend of mine named Glen Basner. We had gone to high school together. When I was shooting *McMullen*, his father had let me use his showroom in the garment district for the scene where McGlone breaks up with his girlfriend. At the time, Glen worked for his father but hated it and wanted to get into the movie business. I helped him get a job as Ted Hope's assistant at Good Machine. An industrious guy, he rose through the ranks in foreign sales.

After a recent promotion, he wanted to bring in a project on his own and called to see what I was up to. We had lunch at Walker's, a neighborhood pub near my office. I gave him *Ash Wednesday*, explaining it was a period piece, set in 1983, and we had it budgeted at $5 million. After reading the script, he said Good Machine was in, they could get the $5 million. Based on that commitment, we went out to actors. Elijah Wood signed on to play opposite me, and we filled out key roles with Oliver Platt and Rosario Dawson. Everything was looking good. We'd be in production soon.

Then I heard from Glen again. They could get us only $2.5 million, half of what we needed to make the movie.

At that point, I probably should have pulled the plug. But I didn't, and I am sure I will make the same mistake again.

Why? Because when I have some money, my script, and my cast, I can see my first shooting day in sight. I want to get on the set. It's that simple. It's too much to resist. So I cut the budget and slashed the number of shooting days. I told myself I could get the job done. I talked to my producers. I talked to my DP. I've made a movie for $25,000. I can certainly make $2.5 million work. Or so I thought.

OUTSIDE OF MY COMFORT ZONE

Before shooting started, I was offered the male lead in *Life or Something Like It*, a romantic comedy starring Angelina Jolie as a TV news reporter looking for meaning in her life. It was a pretty good script, and I wanted to work with Angelina. It was also a very nice paycheck, which is typically the case for a big-budget movie. But it created a conflict. *Life* had a firm start date that overlapped with my own production schedule.

Instead of pushing *Ash Wednesday* and trying to raise more money,

I decided to do both projects. I couldn't help myself. *Ash Wednesday*'s twenty-day shooting schedule was full of challenges. For starters, the movie was set in 1983 and we didn't have the resources to dial back the calendar on camera. On our budget, for instance, we could dress only half the apartment we used for Rosario's home. That meant we could shoot in only one direction. If we had turned around, it would have looked like 2001.

Exteriors were also an issue. We had to shoot with extremely long lenses to hide the fact that we didn't have enough money to close down the street. Shooting with a longer lens keeps your character in focus while everything else in the frame is in soft focus. We used this to mask the present-day buses, cars, and even people who walked through our shots. My first intention had been to shoot handheld, as we had done on *Sidewalks* with great success. Given that we were making a gangster film, we decided to go for a more classic *Godfather/* Gordon Willis look with locked-off compositions (the camera is fixed in one position and doesn't move during the shot) and dramatic, moody light.

However, I believe, the story, the acting, and the energy of the movie as a whole suffered from that choice, and I take full responsibility. Unlike my experience on *Sidewalks*, I could never get the scenes the way I imagined them when I wrote the script. When that happened on my previous low-budget films, I could call an audible. Oh, this scene isn't working? Let's grab the camera, go up on the roof or out to the park, and quickly improvise something. On this film, we couldn't run out to the street corner and sell 1983.

Another problem we encountered was the lead actor. In my previous films, which were all ensembles, I not only played a version of myself, I was also never in more than half the movie. This framework allowed me several days off as an actor during the week.

Those days gave me the opportunity to recharge my batteries and allowed me to focus on the other aspects of filmmaking. So, when I did have to act, capturing the tone and cadence of the characters posed fewer challenges. This time, however, I was playing the lead, where I was in virtually every scene in the film. Moreover, the part of Francis Sullivan, a brooding, deeply conflicted and darker character, required a different amount of preparation and focus, and this eventually took its toll.

Ash Wednesday was also the first movie I wrote that I didn't create bios for each of the characters before writing the script. I don't typically write much character or scene descriptions in my scripts since I am directing and already know the look of the room, the atmosphere, and the other elements writers usually establish. My scripts are very workmanlike. This is the room, here's who is in the room, and this is the dialogue.

What the brevity doesn't reveal is the amount of thought I have put into these characters. I have to know them intimately—their past, their likes and dislikes, their fears and ambitions, everything—before they end up on the page. They need a reason for being there. On *Sidewalks*, I knew those people inside and out. When Dennis Farina read the script, he simply said, "Eddie, I got this guy."

But none of that happened on *Ash Wednesday*. Instead, I was focused on mood and not character. I was a big fan of the dark, somber vibe of Carol Reed's *Odd Man Out* and I wanted the performances to embrace that sense of dread and doom; unfortunately, my characters ended up not feeling real. They were dishonest. They were gangster movie archetypes. Too much brooding and not enough honest human behavior.

On a twenty-day shoot, there is little room for error. We joke now that it was a bad omen when an actress we cast in a pivotal role failed to show up at work on day two of our shoot. The Assistant Director department, which is in charge of scheduling, first called her agents, who then called her apartment, but there was no answer. Our producer, Margot Bridger, went to the actress's apartment. Margot discovered that the actress was dealing with some personal issues and in no shape to work that day. At this point we had already lost half the day and were scrambling to find a replacement. I called a number of actors I knew in New York, hoping to find one who was awake and available to work. Gender was now less important than finding a quality actor on no notice. I quickly did a rewrite in which the character could be a man.

I called a buddy of mine, Jimmy Burke. Jimmy jumped on the train, quickly learned his lines, and saved us that day. But it was a rough way to start.

On top of all that, I was conflicted and distracted every day on the set, knowing I had to show up on *Life or Something Like It* the day after we wrapped. I hurt my own efforts. I think that's why I spent nearly every day debating whether to pull out of the Angelina Jolie movie.

But I couldn't bail only five weeks before the film would shoot. Every time I thought about it, I heard my dad lecturing my brother and me when we were little kids. "Be responsible for your own actions. Think about your choices. Are you going to be an asshole? Or are you going to do the right thing?"

Dailies from *Ash Wednesday* were sent to me in Seattle throughout the production of *Life or Something Like It*. I watched them in my hotel room after work and gave my editor notes over the phone. Every other week, I flew back to New York and we worked together in person. I don't recommend cutting a film that way.

As we edited, I fell in love with the flashback scene that opens

Ash Wednesday. To this day, it's still my favorite part of the movie. It was the only part we shot with a 16 mm handheld camera. I loved the look, the energy, the pace, the intimacy, and the grittiness. The moment I saw it play in the editing room, I knew I had made a mistake not shooting the entire film that way. That is when I decided I was going to remake *Ash Wednesday* one day or at least tell another story of the Irish gangsters who controlled the West Side of New York. (More on that later.)

But here's the thing I've learned about myself. When I make a film, no matter how it eventually turns out, during the process, I love the film. You have to. I think that's true for nearly all filmmakers. You pour yourself into every scene, push yourself to solve countless problems, and as the film comes together in the editing room, with a definitive beginning, middle, and end, you say, "Huh," with a note of surprise. "This works. I love it." Love is blindness.

After *Life* wrapped, I turned my attention back to *Ash Wednesday*. We showed it a couple of times to friends and family, got their notes, and plotted to find distribution. My first step was to make a call to try and get a slot at that year's Sundance Film Festival.

"Look, I haven't been back to the festival since *The Brothers McMullen*. I'd love to come back with my new film."

I sent the film in and waited for a call. Instead, I received a formal letter. It basically said, "Dear Filmmaker, we received your film. Unfortunately, we cannot accept it into the festival."

The rejection itself was painful, but not receiving a personalized letter or a phone call after having once been the toast of the event added salt to the wound. Sure, I was pissed, but it wasn't my first film and it wouldn't be my last.

We then held two distributor screenings that failed to produce a buyer. Finally, Blockbuster purchased the VHS and DVD rights for $500,000—about one-fifth of the production cost. It was something. Typically, this kind of straight-to-video deal meant the film would not play in theaters. However, we were able to convince Blockbuster to allow us a one-weekend theatrical release, in New York and LA, that October.

Not that it mattered. Though the *Los Angeles Times* praised the effort ("suspenseful and ultimately unpredictable, with a sterling ensemble cast"), the majority of other reviewers saw only flaws. In the end, the straight-to-video deal meant *Ash Wednesday* went straight into oblivion. But I was not done with Irish gangsters.

LEGS DIAMOND

I had met author Bill Kennedy through Malachy and Frank Mc-Court at the premiere of *She's the One*. In addition to writing, he taught at SUNY Albany where, if you remember, I nearly failed out of school before getting the advice that changed the course of my life. At his invitation, I screened *No Looking Back* on the SUNY campus and spoke to his students afterward. Later, Bill and I went to dinner, along with former New York governor George Pataki, at a restaurant reputedly frequented by the infamous 1920s Irish American bootlegger Jack "Legs" Diamond.

It was a night of good wine and conversation, and over the course of dinner, Bill and I talked about *Legs*, his acclaimed 1975 novel about Legs Diamond. He had tried to get it made into a movie, he explained, but when it stalled, he did *The Cotton Club* with Francis

Ford Coppola instead. Bill asked if I thought *Legs* would make a good movie, and without any hesitation I said yes, it was one of my favorite novels. We made a plan to adapt the novel together.

I took the first crack, and then Bill went over my draft. We sent drafts back and forth until we felt we had it. In early 2002, we set out to try and get *Legs* made. I attached myself to play the lead role of Legs Diamond (obviously, I hadn't yet learned the lesson from *Ash Wednesday* about being in every scene), and we set out to find the co-lead, Legs's lawyer and confidant, Marcus Gorman.

My producing partner, Aaron, and I knew we had a challenge ahead of us, similar to the one we had with *On the Job*, because this film was a period drama. It was going to be expensive to make. Therefore, we needed a movie star to costar with me. The first two actors we went out to passed in a timely and respectful fashion. As we made an offer to yet another movie star, panic began to set in for Aaron and me.

We had a dispiriting meeting with my representatives, who spoke about the challenges of getting period films made, and we knew *Legs* was dying a slow death. You can feel the posture change from your reps after a couple of passes, and the reality that a film like this is almost impossible to get made without a major movie star. They are a little slower to get back to you on the phone. The discussion is usually steered toward the NBA play-offs or some industry gossip, and a vague plan is offered, usually punting future action weeks down the road. In retrospect, the message is clear: It's time to spend your energy on a new project.

When the writing is on the wall, Aaron and I move off the project quickly. This is when I start writing a new script, hoping to fall out of love with the old one. It helps, but it may not always be the best strategy, and sometimes perseverance on one project can and will pay off. There are those movies like *Dallas Buyers Club*, which can take two decades to get made. That said, being on the offense and making a movie is our goal. We can always pull out that old script down the road and bring it into the marketplace with a rewrite or a new spin to make it feel fresh.

However, after *Legs*, I was disappointed that my two dream genres, period cop and gangster movies, were dreams unfulfilled.

TEN

CONFIDENCE

After the disappointment of *Ash Wednesday* and the holding pattern *Legs* was placed in, I decided I would finally listen to the advice of my agents and throw my hat into the acting ring for real. I would focus on acting and only acting, and I promised myself I wouldn't distract myself by writing a screenplay. Truthfully, I was gun-shy and wasn't sure what to do about my writing and directing career.

One of the first scripts my agents sent was a screenplay called *Confidence*, written by a first-time screenwriter named Doug Jung. The script was a page-turner, clearly inspired by the great noir films made decades ago, but with a modern edge. The characters and dialogue popped, and the opportunity to play the ringleader of the con men was irresistible.

I flew out to Los Angeles for a meeting with director James Foley (whose directing résumé included *At Close Range, Fear,* and *Glengarry Glen Ross*) to discuss playing the part of con man Jake Vig. Everything about this project felt right. I loved the script, which told the story of a career con artist (Vig) who gets mixed up with the mob. Foley was another Irish guy from New York who ended up in the movie biz, and we bonded immediately. A few days after the meeting, I got the offer.

I flew back to New York feeling pretty great. I was the lead in a very cool movie with a very good filmmaker.

Foley was attracting an incredible cast that included Rachel Weisz, Andy Garcia, Paul Giamatti, Luis Guzmán, and Donal Logue. When he had trouble casting the movie's villain, a tough mob chieftain, I suggested looking for a great actor who normally didn't get offered the tough guy role. I mentioned Dustin Hoffman as that type of actor, and Foley immediately jumped on the idea. Dustin loved the script and loved Foley. Dustin even created his hyperactive, gum-chewing gangster character based loosely on Foley.

"I watched the director because I like the director," explains Hoffman. "There were certain things about him I thought would be fun. He chewed gum incessantly and the first meeting we had he was wearing a black shirt, black pants and he had glasses around his neck. I said, 'Can I borrow your glasses?' I put his glasses on, and I said, 'Do you have any gum? Could you take your shirt off?' and I just literally put on his clothing.

"James also has a very fast rhythm. He talks very fast, very fast—even faster than I did in the film. So that's how I found King."

Jo Manning, *The Free Library*

Getting the opportunity to work with Dustin is one of the great thrills of my career. Talking with him about *The Graduate* and *Midnight Cowboy*, two of my all-time favorite movies, and the classic *All the President's Men* was more insightful than any film studies class I took in college. Like my experience working opposite De Niro in *15 Minutes*, I used the opportunity to pick Hoffman's brain. Any actor wants to get better at his or her craft, and I tried to use these opportunities as a chance to improve my game. If *Saving Private Ryan* was my graduate school for directing, then the same could be said of watching Dustin every day on the set of *Confidence*.

I think it paid off. As far as I was concerned, it was the best acting I had done to date. Being on Foley's set and focusing solely on acting proved to be an eye-opener for me. This was the first time I wasn't also working on a script in my trailer between scenes. In fact, it was the first time I was not writing a screenplay in my adult life. Why have that kind of headache if I could have an easier time of it as an actor? I told my agents I wanted to act for the next few years. I didn't want to think about writing or making films. I was now ready to throw myself headfirst into my acting career.

My team couldn't be happier. They had been begging me to do this for a few years. Go try and be a movie star, they would argue. You can make your little indie movies when you're old and fat and you've lost your hair.

They immediately sent over the script for *A Sound of Thunder*, a sci-fi movie based on a 1952 Ray Bradbury story about a modern-day hunter who travels back in time to hunt a Tyrannosaurus rex.

The film would shoot right on the heels of *Confidence* that summer in Prague. The timing was perfect and the financial offer they made me was even better. The producers were offering a ton of money, more than double any payday I had gotten before.

I had my concerns about the script, but when I met with the director, Peter Hyams, he delivered a passionate explanation about his vision for the movie. He talked about the special effects he envisioned, and the work he was going to do on the screenplay. It was a great speech, and Peter did a top-notch job selling it, as one must when pitching a movie to financiers, producers, and actors. I walked out of his office and called my agents. "Let's do it."

I signed on, and a mere three days after *Confidence* wrapped, I got on a plane to Prague. Once there, I met the other leads, Ben Kingsley and Catherine McCormack, two extremely talented and experienced actors. This movie was going to be another great learning experience and I was excited to start this new phase of my career.

I was going to chase this movie star thing. I had my first real payday and I didn't have to worry about editing, distribution, or paying back investors.

I had a good time making the movie, working with these terrific actors, and living in a great European city for a couple of months. But something was missing. Maybe I just missed New York City, my home. But if I was being honest, what I really missed was being a filmmaker.

WHAT NEXT?

Confidence was scheduled to come out in April, and Lionsgate and Foley were over the moon about the film. Everyone was convinced they had a big hit on their hands. The film would premiere at Sundance and I'd be returning to the festival for the first time since *McMullen*.

Then I got a call from Harvey Weinstein, the influential, opinionated, and very smart cofounder of Miramax Films. Through

Miramax, Harvey and his brother, Bob, had given the indie film business box-office clout and taken it to Oscar-winning heights in the eighties and nineties.

It was shortly before the holidays, and Harvey's call was unexpected. His voice was upbeat, enthusiastic.

"Eddie, I just saw you in *Confidence*," he said. "I want you to promise me one thing—that you're not going to make any independent movies for the next five years. You need to go and be a movie star."

I didn't know what to say. It was both a compliment and a critique of my career in the same breath. But you know what, I was up for being a movie star, and if that's what Harvey thought, well, Harvey's thoughts mattered to people in the business. After that call, I felt like I was doing the right thing. Sit tight and wait for that right next role.

In January 2003, I joined James Foley at the Sundance Film Festival. Sitting there with Foley, Dustin Hoffman, Andy Garcia, and Paul Giamatti, listening to the applause as the lights came up, was as good as it gets. It was one of those special nights you get in this business. You're celebrating with a group of people you admire and enjoying the rewards of your hard work. As I stood on the stage with Hollywood royalty, I couldn't help but think back to being there at Sundance eight years earlier. This is where my career started, and I savored the moment.

All of us left Sundance believing the movie was going to be a big hit. I agreed to countless meetings but still couldn't find the next acting job that felt right. My team at CAA advised me to wait for *Confidence* to open. They were sure the movie would pop and better offers would stream in. Unfortunately, we had to wait four more months until *Confidence* reached theaters. When it was finally released in April 2003, we found ourselves up against John Cusack's horror film *Identity*, and it kicked our ass.

Confidence underperformed. Despite some rave reviews, it didn't make any money. And like that, my acting career screeched to a halt. I was given my leading-man shots: a movie with De Niro, a movie with Angelina Jolie, and a movie with Dustin Hoffman, and none of them made a dime. I knew my movie with Ben Kingsley was destined for the straight-to-DVD-bin at the video store. Those are the four nails in the proverbial coffin. I had a feeling I wouldn't be hearing from Harvey Weinstein any time soon.

It was hard for me to get too upset. I'm a realist. Shit happens. I knew a couple of things had thwarted my climb to movie stardom. First, I had a little bit of bad luck. The movies with the big name costars should have been hits. They should have been at least doubles. Instead, they were strikeouts. And second, to be a movie star, you have to really want to be a movie star. You have to work at it. You should move to Los Angeles, and then you have to fight tooth and nail for those acting jobs. It's very competitive at the top. But I never wanted to be Paul Newman, I wanted to be Woody Allen. I have always been more interested in stealing away to my trailer between scenes to work on a screenplay. That's not the sign of the guy who loves acting; that's the sign of the guy who loves writing.

So as I had done in the past, it was time to be in charge of my own destiny. That's how I got into independent film in the first place. I suppose it's the core trait for being independent.

GOING DIGITAL

I wanted to make a New York movie and I wanted to write something Adam Goldberg and I could do together. We had talked about making a movie since becoming friends on *Saving Private Ryan*. I had made a number of movies that explored the relationships between fathers and sons, and I also wanted to tackle the relationship between mothers and their sons.

With that in mind, I came up with *Mothers and Sons*, the story of two successful New York women who were best friends, and their adult sons who, unlike their mothers, never really liked each other but have always found themselves forced together by their overbearing moms.

As everyone knows, the quality roles for women over the age of forty are few and far between in Hollywood films, let alone for women in their late fifties. We made offers to two legends, Mia Farrow and Sally Field, who both signed on immediately. The great thing about casting two fantastic actresses like Mia and Sally is that they attracted other terrific actors. We soon added Griffin Dunne, Sam Elliott, Julia Louis-Dreyfus, and Christina Ricci to our ensemble.

We budgeted *Mothers and Sons* at $6 million and took it out.

We immediately got a bite from Fox Searchlight. I spoke with Peter Rice, the company's president, on a Thursday. He said he was halfway through the script and loving it.

"We'll let you know on Monday," he said.

I was ecstatic. It seemed like I would be back at the studio where I began my career.

On Monday, my agents called. Fox Searchlight passed.

Eventually, Lionsgate offered $2 million for the domestic rights. Though they liked the script and our cast, they didn't think domestic was worth more. Our agents at William Morris then tried to raise the rest of the budget through foreign sales, with no luck.

Having learned my lessons from *Ash Wednesday*, I wasn't going to try and make this film on a lower budget. And so another script went into the drawer.

By then, the summer was almost over and I didn't have anything lined up. Nor had I done anything since finishing *A Sound of Thunder* nearly a year earlier. I feared I had been put in director's jail after going eight years without equaling the success of my first movie. My acting career seemed to have deposited me in a kind of exile, too.

I was nervous. I was going to be thirty-five years old, and my first child was due in October. I was no longer the young kid in the business, and for the first time in my career, I didn't have a plan.

Then one day while riding the 1 train uptown, I saw a guy wearing an official crew sweatshirt for the movie *Jungle Fever*. On the sleeve was a patch that read FIVE IN FIVE, FIVE FILMS IN FIVE YEARS. I liked that. That had always been my dream, to make one movie a year like Woody Allen has done for the last forty years. I decided then that, like Spike and Woody, I was going to try and make a movie a year as a filmmaker. And that's what I set out to do. I was going to make a movie that year, come hell or high water.

Then I read an article about the movies *Tadpole* and *Pieces of April*. The first had come out the previous year while I was busy acting and it had sailed under my radar. The second was screening around New York just prior to its release in theaters. Both were produced by my former attorney, John Sloss, whom I'm now lucky enough to be working with again. He had started InDigEnt—Independent Digital Entertainment—with director Gary Winick and several others who saw new digital cameras as an opportunity to rethink the way indie movies could be made and financed. Some directors were going into production without a full script. They were casting people who improvised. They didn't bother writing scenes as much as they created them on the spot. Since they were shooting digitally, they didn't have to worry about the high cost of film. They could shoot as much as they wanted, then piece it together later.

Their mentality was the opposite of those in Hollywood looking to make the next blockbuster. Deals were cut with the unions so that crews were small and costs were kept very low, around $200,000 or less. These guys were getting films made and released—and some were even making money.

At the end of the day, that was the point—to do something I loved and make enough money to do it again. My twelve days.

The first movie shot with a digital camera that got my attention was *The Celebration* from the Danish Dogme 95 movement. Dogme 95 was a filmmaking style born of directors Lars Von Trier and Thomas Vinterberg and based on bare-bones, natural production values. *The Celebration* was shot with a Sony DCR-PC7E Handycam. Digital minicassettes replaced film.

Both *Tadpole* and *Pieces of April* were New York movies, and both were shot with a Panasonic 24p, one of the first digital cameras that provided a more filmic look. I spoke with John Sloss and learned that his company had worked out a deal with the unions allowing filmmakers to employ them at a lower-budget level. Aaron and I agreed. We could make a movie for $200,000.

ELEVEN

LOOKING FOR KITTY

During Christy's last few weeks of pregnancy, I started to outline a new movie idea. After our daughter, Grace, arrived in October, I started to write *Looking for Kitty*, a comedy-drama about a private detective hired by a baseball coach to find his runaway wife. The script was loose, more outline than script. I sat in front of my laptop, writing myself a job as much as I was writing a story. I wanted to get back in the game, to get back behind the camera, to work with actor friends who could, hopefully, improvise.

Obviously, I wasn't concerned about writing a great screenplay. I was more excited about getting to play with this new digital approach. I just wanted to get outside and make another movie. And that's what we did.

While writing the script, I came across a book about architectural holdouts from New York City's past, relics owned by people who wouldn't sell to developers buying up the rest of the block. The pictures of old buildings dwarfed by modern towers gave me an idea for my character. I made him a holdout, a detective who was stuck in time. As the world went digital, he stayed old-school.

Despite more sophisticated ways to spy on someone, he prefers to wait outside their apartment in his car, then follow them "like Bogie would," as my character explains. For backstory, I imagined his wife had died years earlier and his life had stopped there. Then our detective gets this case from a small-town guy, a baseball coach from Upstate New York. His wife is missing, and he needs the detective's help finding her.

I got David Krumholtz for the role of the baseball coach. As the story progresses, our characters discover his wife isn't missing. She has gone to New York City to see a show. While looking for clues, my character finds a picture of her in a magazine that links her to a middle-aged rock star. Max Baker took on that part. And *Saturday Night Live* regulars Rachel Dratch and Chris Parnell added a dose of genuine funny to the cast.

The fifteen-day shoot, done in the dead of winter, was no-frills. Our $200,000 budget was considerably more than *McMullen*, but still, by indie film standards, this was bare-bones. We didn't have trailers, hair and makeup, catering, or many of the other perks that are taken for granted on a traditional movie set. Everyone did everything; cast and crew alike lugged lights and equipment. It was a miserable, hard experience because of the weather. Put simply, we froze our asses off. However, I made sure lunch was first class. Every day, we picked the nicest restaurant near where we were shooting, ordered great bottles of wine, and sat together for two hours (we had heard that French movie crews did this) at one long table, eating, laughing, and talking about film.

As I began looking at dailies, I found that the digital camera didn't impress me. Though I liked the way the small camera let us steal shots around Times Square and on subways without attracting any attention, the footage looked foggy and muddy. Digital cinema still had a long way to go, but that was the least of our problems.

As we put the movie together in postproduction, I discovered an issue with the tone. *Looking for Kitty* contained elements from two different types of movies. I wanted to walk the line between broad comedy and more realistic dramatic moments. The films that can execute that most honestly reflect everyday life. I felt I was able to achieve that balance in *The Brothers McMullen*, *She's the One,* and, most successfully, *Sidewalks of New York.* It's a tricky thing to pull off, which is why you don't see it too often. There are dramas and there are comedies, but my favorite films have been those that manage to do both. I think back to that very first film I saw in my film appreciation class at SUNY Albany—Billy Wilder's *The Apartment.* The screenplay and the performances of Jack Lemmon and Shirley MacLaine, guided by Wilder's direction, beautifully walked the line between comedy and drama. *Looking for Kitty* did not.

There are some touching, nice moments in the film and there are some laughs, but I know the reason the film ultimately didn't work was that I went into production without a completed screenplay. Had we set out to make a comedy, maybe we could have gotten away with this more improvised approach, but the tone we were trying to achieve needed to be carefully calibrated; it isn't achieved willy-nilly.

The best part of *Looking for Kitty* is evident in the credits. Listed there are the names of the crew I still work with today: My DP, Will Rexer, has shot every film I've made since. At our first meeting, I learned he was a new dad like me, lived in Tribeca, and loved the same movies. We talked Antonioni and De Sica, Coppola and

Scorsese, Truffaut and Rohmer. Within a day, I knew we were going to be friends for the rest of our lives.

I first met my longtime composer, P. T. Walkley, at Ludlow Guitars on the Lower East Side while we were shooting *Kitty*. My wife had given me guitar lessons as a birthday present, and P.T. was one of my teachers. One day I mentioned I was making a low-budget movie and didn't have money for music.

He said, "Why don't I give you my demo?"

He did, and I loved it. P.T. joined forces with Robert Gary, another guitar teacher at the shop, and they did the score for *Kitty* and my follow-up film, *The Groomsmen*. P.T. has been doing the music for all my films since.

I also met another member of our filmmaking family, Janet Gaynor, the editor of my last four projects since *Kitty*. At the time, she was an assistant editor to Sarah Flack, who had recently cut Sofia Coppola's *Lost in Translation* and was cutting *Kitty*.

We were also introduced to a young Canadian named Mike Harrop, who offered to be our postproduction supervisor. Mike was another invaluable member of our team, and as we did more projects, he started working on the production end of things as well as post, ultimately line producing our three microbudget films.

By most standards, *Looking for Kitty* was a failure. At one point, I even told Aaron that we shouldn't finish the film, just shelve it. I even regretted making the movie. But years later, after a great screening at the Toronto Film Festival of *The Fitzgerald Family Christmas*, a film we all collaborated on, I was reminded that Will Rexer, P. T. Walkley, Janet Gaynor, Mike Harrop, Aaron Lubin, and I all first worked together on *Looking for Kitty*. It's then I realized that there are no mistakes. And there are no bad films. Making movies is a gift, it's a joy. We laughed our asses off on the set of *Kitty* and we were still laughing our asses off that night eight years later. You're not going to hear too many stories like that in the film business. There is a misguided notion that you must suffer for the work, but it doesn't have to be that way. The work is hard, that's true, but at the end of the day, you're only making a movie. It's a privilege to make a movie, and I never forget that.

A couple thoughts for the first-time filmmaker: If you allow yourself to get crippled by the possibility of failure, you're going to rob yourself of a lot of great experiences. There are very few great films, but something great, be it a new actor relationship or learning a new technology, has always come from my experiences making films, even if the film itself was disappointing. Additionally, consider how you can empower people who are working for peanuts. *Looking for Kitty* lists eight people as producers or coproducers, including Aaron and myself. Why so many? We give out producer credits as perks to people who work mostly on the promise of a percentage of profits. Everyone has skin in the game. Find skilled, talented people willing to share a vision and work shoulder to shoulder doing whatever it takes to make the film a go. It's a collaborative business. If they help produce, make them producers.

Looking for Kitty got into the Tribeca Film Festival. It played okay. But I left the theater that night worried about the film's prospects. I read the room and knew better than to trust the compliments I received after the lights went on. You have to be careful with festival screenings. They are the friendliest audiences you are going to find, and sometimes the laughter and applause aren't an accurate read.

This was one of those times. The phone didn't ring. When I checked in with my agent to see if he'd had any calls from potential distributors, he said no, adding that no news was exactly what it was, no news—which, from my perspective, was bad news.

How do you deal with that? Fall in love with a new set of characters and a new screenplay. I found it's always easier to deal with the disappointment of a bad review or a soft opening weekend at the box office when you're already consumed with the new script you're working on. When you are deep into the writing process, you start to see the movie in your head. When you can see the movie in your head, you want to see the movie on-screen. That's where your focus goes. So I knew what I had to do. Start writing.

I never really stop writing. There is always an idea I'm working on; sometimes it's just an outline or a handful of scenes. These ideas, whether they are fully fleshed out or just character sketches, float around in the back of your head and then one day jump into the forefront. You can't shake the idea or the character. You're on the subway, you're at a bar, you're having dinner with friends, and your thoughts are drawn back to the idea. At this point, I go into investigative mode. I start picking people's brains. It may sound like casual conversation but I'm doing my research. I'm developing my characters' backstory. I ask friends and family their opinion on whatever subject I'm exploring. I implore them to share stories from their own lives that I may be able to use as inspiration or in some cases steal, with their permission of course.

I was still searching for the next script idea while having dinner with my wife one night. Christy and I had been married about a year at this point and we were laughing about some of the headaches we had to deal with and the negotiations we had to make with friends and family when we were planning our wedding.

Christy then said, "You know that goofy script you wrote about the guy and the girl, they're planning a wedding, and she's pregnant?" I nodded. "You should go back and redo that one. Write the real version of it."

I had written a few drafts of a script called *The Groomsmen* a few years earlier. It follows a group of guys in the days before one of them gets married. The guys still feel, and often act, like twenty-two-year-olds, when suddenly they face their own change-of-life crises and have to figure out some of life's important questions, such as marriage, commitment, fatherhood, and friendship.

When I first conceived this script, I was trying to write something funny and broad in the vein of *Meet the Parents* and *Old School*. Two films I loved and two films that were rewarded at the box office. I was hoping my next film would do the same. The early drafts of my script were pretty good but fell apart in the third act, as happens with a lot of comedies. You have to go big and ridiculous at the end. I tried, but I quickly realized I didn't know how to write that kind of comedy. It just isn't my sensibility. And like so many other screenplays I'd written, *The Groomsmen* went in the drawer. I'd return to it one day when the inspiration struck, and that night at dinner with my wife, it did.

I decided my rewrite would steer away from a mainstream comedy; I would try for a more honest representation of men in their midthirties struggling to mature. I looked to Fellini's 1953 masterpiece *I Vitelloni* for inspiration. It's the story of five carefree guys plotting and dreaming of life beyond their small Italian town. Aaron and I had long conversations about how the script should explore the different definitions of what it meant to be a man. Like a lot of guys in their thirties, we had friends who were holding on to their adolescence, unwilling to grow up, and terrified of the future. We also had friends who had graduated successfully into adulthood, who were husbands and fathers. We wanted to explore all the shades in between. In essence, we were looking to make a coming-of-age movie that addressed this new-threshold moment.

After sending the finished screenplay to my agents, we met to discuss how we were going to put financing together for *The Groomsmen*. With the script and a list of actors in front of me, we mapped out our strategy.

At Aaron's suggestion, we got Jay Mohr to play one of the key supporting roles. As soon as his name came up, I knew he'd be perfect, and he was. I always pictured Donal Logue, who was sensational in *Confidence*, as the older brother; and we got him, too. Then Matthew Lillard read the script and wanted to play Dez, the role I had envisioned for myself. Matt was passionate about the role, so much so that I agreed to let him take the part of Dez, and I stepped into the role of Paulie.

Though we still hadn't finished casting, we gave the script to CAA and went out with it. A few weeks later, we found ourselves up against the wall again. They couldn't get the movie financed.

Then, after a couple of weeks of limbo, they had somebody who wanted in. Suddenly, all was not lost. His name was Philippe Martinez. He was a Frenchman with a theater background who had moved to Montreal to get into the movie business. Since 1999, he'd had his own company, Bauer Martinez Studios.

Apparently, he was a fan of mine. Word came back that *The Groomsmen* reminded him of *The Brothers McMullen*, and he wanted to fully finance the movie at $3 million.

"He wants to know if you can meet him in New York," my agent said.

Aaron and I met Philippe at a Tribeca restaurant called the Harrison. He explained he had made his share of B movies but had also, in this latest chapter of his company, worked with Andy Garcia, Jeff Bridges, and Ralph Fiennes. He was committed to backing real storytellers. That was how he envisioned making a bigger mark—with smaller, auteur-driven films. He wanted to make ten a year in the $3 million to $5 million range.

"We're committed to this type of film," he explained. "If one of them hits, we're in great shape."

By the end of the meal, the three of us shook hands and agreed to make the movie together. First up, we needed to finish casting. We needed my character's wife and our final groomsmen. Philippe suggested John Leguizamo for the part of T.C., which I thought was a great idea. Fortunately for us, John said yes and is terrific in the movie, playing a character who, upon his return home, confesses to his childhood friends that he is gay.

Philippe insisted that in order to finance the movie, he would need a big name for the female lead. I knew this would be a challenge, given that it was a smaller, supporting role. If I was going to get this movie made, I would need to call in a favor. So I called Brittany Murphy, who I had worked with years earlier on *Sidewalks of New York*, and begged her to do the film for me. I promised her I could get her in and out in a week.

I said, "You'll start on a Monday and go home on a Friday."

She joined our cast without hesitation. Brittany was a great kid and a wonderful actress. Her passing was a tragic loss. We all loved working with her and still miss her spirit.

With John and Brittany on board, Bauer Martinez started

cash-flowing our film almost immediately. Our deal wasn't even finished and we went into production.

It was spring, a wonderful time to make a movie in New York. The weather was great, everyone got along, and we all felt good about the work. We shot in all five boroughs—in twenty-five days—with the bulk of it on City Island in the Bronx. Twenty-five days is a tight schedule but it never felt like we were rushing. That was due largely in part to Margot Bridger.

I should take time here to talk about Margot, another key member of my filmmaking family. When Michael Nozik, my former producer on *She's the One* and *No Looking Back*, was unavailable to produce *Sidewalks of New York*, I asked him if he knew any great New York–based producers. Michael told me that he did in fact know someone I would love. He said that his former assistant and protégé, Margot Bridger, would be perfect to produce *Sidewalks*, especially given that we were aiming to make that movie for $1 million. Margot and I clicked on day one, and she would go on to produce four more films with us. Simply, there is no better producer in New York City at making sure every dollar gets on-screen. Even though *The Groomsmen* was a $3 million movie, we never felt rushed or under the gun. We had all the toys a studio filmmaker would want at his disposal: Steadicams, cranes, and for our final shot on the Staten Island Ferry, a helicopter. These things don't happen on a $3 million movie unless you have an excellent producer fighting for every last dollar. It's a lesson she taught Aaron that we still refer to every time he and I review a production budget.

Aaron and Margot would share an office, and Aaron remembers calling to arrange a drum lesson for Jay Mohr because his character plays drums. The cost of the lesson was $75. Margot, overhearing the call, asked Aaron how we were going to pay for it.

After all, she said, "It's not in the budget."

Aaron responded, "But Jay's character needs to know how to play drums."

Margot asked, "But how are we going to pay for it?"

Aaron shrugged, thinking it would all "come out in the wash."

Margot and Aaron laughed. They both knew that on a movie, things don't come out in the wash. Instead, you go over budget and over schedule. The harder job is finding that $75 from somewhere else. On every movie we've done with Margot, we've never gone a day over schedule or a dollar over budget.

The Groomsmen was no exception. We came in on budget and on schedule. Postproduction, steered by Mike Harrop, went as smoothly as the shooting had, and we locked picture a few months later. It was now time to take the movie out to LA and test it in front of an audience, where the other shoe finally dropped.

The screening was at the Galleria movie complex in Sherman Oaks, California. This is where I very nearly came to blows with a marketing consultant that Bauer Martinez had hired when we tested *The Groomsmen* in front of an audience. After the screening, as the test scores were tallied, this guy came up to me and began telling me about the movie. I had never met or seen him before. Suddenly, he was lecturing me.

"You have to cut the scene in the strip club. Women don't want to see a scene in a strip club."

He hadn't even introduced himself, so right away, he's dead to me.

I ignored him, but he didn't get it. The moment there was a lull in the conversation, he jumped in again.

"Who the fuck is this guy?"

It didn't matter. I pivoted around and looked directly into his eyes.

"Look, I don't know who you are, so your opinion about what I need to do or cut doesn't matter to me."

He wagged his finger at me.

"Get your fucking finger out of my face," I said.

At that point, Aaron stepped between us. He realized no one else was going to intervene, and if that were the case, this guy was soon going to be lights-out in the aisle of the theater. Aaron diffused the situation by getting me out of the theater. For the next three days, he fielded phone calls from the Bauer Martinez team, who was asking what had happened and how I felt. At first, I wanted a pound of flesh. Aaron talked me down. Instead of getting even, he said, let's get something from them. "This is an opportunity. If you need something from them or want something, now is the time to ask."

What we needed was final cut. I also needed assurance from Philippe that he was still committed to making Bauer Martinez a filmmaker-friendly company. That meant listening to the opinion of his filmmakers over his marketing consultants. I explained how I wanted *The Groomsmen* to succeed as much as he did. I told him I had no interest in making a dark drama, and I asked him to have faith that I would deliver a movie with plenty of laughs and an uplifting ending. Still, I needed to keep some of the darker, more dramatic scenes in the film, including the strip club scene. To Philippe's credit, he agreed and we shook on it. A summer 2006 release date was penciled in.

Philippe had ambitious plans for Bauer Martinez. Not only was the company fully financing feature films, but instead of taking those films out into the acquisitions marketplace to find distribution, Philippe decided to launch his own distribution company. Within a year, he and his team hired a distribution staff, marketing personnel, and a publicity department, in the hopes of competing with the

Weinstein Company, Fox Searchlight, and all the other specialized distribution companies. I'm sure they'd agree that they'd bit off more than they could chew.

That said, Bauer Martinez did a surprisingly good job with our marketing materials. They cut together a charming trailer and designed a poster that we felt accurately represented the tone of the movie, which is rarely the case. However, a year later, when the film was released on DVD, the home entertainment company Universal Music Group decided to go in a very different direction with the artwork. Let's just say we were not happy.

In April, *The Groomsmen* premiered at the fifth Tribeca Film Festival. As I read the vibe in the theater, our July theatrical release started to look even better. I felt we had at least a single, maybe a double, and beyond that, who knew.

Events played out differently than I had hoped. On July 14, *The Groomsmen* opened with a fifty-screen limited release across the country. It was buoyed by reviews that ranged from a friendly nod in *Entertainment Weekly* ("Every actor registers") to an endorsement from the *San Francisco Chronicle* ("This is like any other Edward Burns film, except for one thing. It's unmistakably better").

The glaring problem was that Bauer Martinez had no experience in distributing a specialized movie (indies are considered specialized releases). Typically, these films are given a platform release, opening in NYC and LA and then expanding to other markets the following few weeks. A deft strategy is employed that usually involves working with key art house theater owners as well as the preeminent journalists who cover specialized movies. It's important to get the right placement and press, while also applying the right amount of pressure with the key exhibitors to keep the movie playing. Bauer Martinez just didn't have the experience to do either and with a nickel-and-dime

Me and Johnny Legs rocking on City Island in the Bronx

marketing budget (the average cost to market a film for theatrical release in 2005 was $35 million and I believe we were about $35 million shy of that), we never stood a chance at the box office.

The movie was out of theaters several weeks later and grossed $128,000. A disproportionate amount of those sales were generated from New York City, where I had been to numerous Q&As at the theaters. Like many other specialized distribution companies, Bauer Martinez was rudely awakened to the economic realities of that arena and ultimately closed their distribution company after releasing only a few films. Following on our heels at Bauer Martinez was a Richard Gere–Claire Danes thriller and a Paul Rudd–Michelle Pfeiffer romantic comedy, both of which had budgets around $30 million. Neither of these movies were released theatrically. The silver lining for *The Groomsmen* was that we at least made it to theaters.

Oscar-winning film and sound editor Walter Murch said it best: "You can always make a film somehow. You can beg, borrow, steal the equipment, use credit cards, use your friends' goodwill, wheedle your way into this or that situation. The real problem is, how do you get people to see it once it is made?" You play the cards you're dealt, and in terms of financing, Bauer Martinez delivered on everything we needed to make the movie, but their decision to distribute it destined the movie to fail theatrically. And that was just bad luck. The last time I'd worked with a brand-new distribution company was on *McMullen*, and they knocked it out of the park. Hard work is required in this business, tenacity is a must, and talent will always help your cause. However, you're not going to get anywhere without a little bit of good luck. I had it with *McMullen* and it didn't come my way with *The Groomsmen*, but I had been at it long enough to know that action was the answer.

THIRTEEN
PURPLE VIOLETS

t was now 2005 and we had done two films in two years. I knew that in order to make another film the following year, I had to get writing.

I had an idea for a film about an enormously successful writer of crime novels who has everything one could want except critical acclaim. He craves to be acknowledged as an esteemed novelist. When he finally does write the book that he believes is his masterpiece, the critics trash it. After reading the reviews, he walks out the back door of his beautiful Hamptons beach house, jumps into the ocean, swims out, and the movie ends. I never wrote the script, but I did like the idea of the writer who wrestles with that dilemma. Do you write the story that comes from the heart, or do you write the story that pays the bills? I had gotten lucky with *The Brothers McMullen*, as that film satisfied both goals, but it had been a long time since one of my films found any real commercial success, and this debate was beginning to consume me. I decided that my next script would explore that tough decision.

Purple Violets is the story of two novelists who were former lovers at NYU and reunite in their late thirties. My protagonist, Patti, is a writer who has put her career on hold after the publication of a critically acclaimed short-story collection. She now doesn't write for fear that she can't match her previous success. Patti crosses paths with her college sweetheart, Brian, a successful writer of crime novels in search of literary credibility.

Once Patti and Brian reconnect, it forces their respective best friends, Michael and Kate, to get back in touch. Their issues are as passionate as they were twenty years earlier.

It was a familiar construct for me. It enabled me to look at the way relationships you have in your formative years maintain a hold on you later on. There was romance and sex, drama and comedy. But there was also a serious undercurrent. Nearly all the conversations between the two main characters, Brian and Patti, are about the cost of creating personal work from the heart versus the pursuit of more commercial success. Which was the way to go?

The theme I was looking to explore was the idea of second chances. Would Brian get his shot at literary acclaim? Would Patti ever write another book? Would the other two characters in the film, Kate and Michael, get another chance at love?

"There are no second acts," my character, Michael, tells Brian in one scene, quoting F. Scott Fitzgerald.

"I don't believe that, and neither do you," Brian replies.

In a way, I was thinking out loud and wondering the same about my career. Was there a second act in store for me?

Every film is its own mountain of challenges, an uphill climb full of exhilarating moments, self-doubt, hope, disappointment, hard work, laughs, mistakes, and even some triumphs. Such is this business. You want to make movies. The desire and passion burns in your blood. You don't have a choice. Making movies isn't what you do, it's who you are. But it's just so hard to get them made, and then even harder to get them seen. If it's too hard for you, you're in the wrong business. If you like running into brick walls, stick with it. I knew if I wanted a second act for my career, I needed to be the architect of it, and that meant I needed to figure out a way to continue making movies.

We put together a cast that included Patrick Wilson and Selma Blair for the leads, Brian and Patti. I played Michael, Brian's best friend and attorney, and Donal Logue committed to playing Patti's controlling husband. Debra Messing flew east from LA to play Patti's best friend, Kate, who was my character's girlfriend in college—until I cheated on her. We also cast good friend and hysterically funny Dennis Farina. Ever the trouper, Dennis banged out several scenes in one day. He is sorely missed.

We had budgeted the picture at $4 million but had not yet raised any money. I wanted my cast in place before I went looking for money.

Pamela Schein Murphy, a woman I met through friends in New York, wanted to get into the movie business. I spoke to her about the ins and outs of financing, and soon we had a backer for *Purple Violets*. Pam's company, Lucky Day Pictures, agreed to finance the film, and *Purple Violets* began shooting in and around Lower Manhattan.

Every day was fun. Aaron, DP Will Rexer, and I relished the comfort. On *Ash Wednesday*, we had shot in shitty bars and tiny apartments, and we had made *Looking for Kitty* outdoors in the dead of a freezing winter. By contrast, *Purple Violets* was set in big, airy lofts, gorgeous restaurants, and beautiful tree-lined streets.

Of all my films, *Purple Violets* is where I was most successful in featuring the city as a supporting character. That happened organically, as a result of the ease and enjoyment we had making the movie. In those situations, you let yourself go with the vibe, and I did. This project was the third film that Will Rexer and I had collaborated on. Even though it was a twenty-five-day schedule, we had to move quickly and there were some days that were run-and-gun in nature. We also knew we had the opportunity to experiment with the camera. I mentioned earlier when talking about *She's the One* that I am an admirer of Woody Allen's moving masters. These long, single takes where the camera doesn't cut, sometimes for the entire length of the scene, were a staple of Woody's, and a big part of why I was drawn to the filmmaker's work. Will and I identified a number of scenes in the *Purple Violets* script where we wanted to embrace that cinematic style and create the kind of shots that we admired in those films. There are a few scenes in Selma Blair's apartment where we executed these shots beautifully.

Shooting a scene with a moving master is always a great challenge for both the cast and crew. For the cast, it's more like performing onstage. Typically when shooting a film, if an actor forgets a line or isn't happy with their performance, they know they'll not only get another take but there will be other shots from various angles (e.g., medium shot, close-up, etc.) where that line will be covered. However, if you forget or flub a line when shooting a three-minute moving master, the entire take is no good.

The same holds true for the crew. These shots are carefully choreographed so that the character's blocking (where/how the actor moves around a space) works for the camera's position, angle, and focus. If the dolly or Steadicam accidentally bumps into a piece of furniture, or the boom microphone enters the shot, or the camera assistant loses focus because the actor doesn't stop exactly where rehearsed, the shot is blown. Usually, these types of shots take a long time to set up and a long time to rehearse. But if you get it right once, you're done with the scene.

Purple Violets really was one of those charmed shoots. It was fall in New York, and we were making a movie with an experienced crew, many of whom were friends and longtime collaborators. In addition, we had an excellent cast of gung ho, up-for-anything actors, and a filmmaking-friendly financier and producer. We were having fun, living the dream.

When we finished shooting, Aaron and I went out for a drink. We knew we had done good work and we felt we finally had a movie that would get us over the hump. Our new editor, Thom Zimny, had been raving about the footage and when we settled into the editing room, we could see why. The actors delivered and Will's photography was gorgeous. For $4 million, we had a New York romantic comedy that looked like a studio film.

P. T. Walkley produced a beautiful score, and when we screened the film for our agents at CAA in Los Angeles, everyone was confident we finally had a hit on our hands. An agent of mine had been trying for years to convince me to abandon my small, personal films and throw my hat in the studio directing world. After screening *Purple Violets*, he shook my hand and told me, "I loved it and I promise I'll never try to dissuade you from making your small movies again."

At the end of 2005, I had three movies in the can. I was convinced 2006 was going to be a good year. *The Groomsmen* had not been released yet, and *Purple Violets* was our best work to date. I believed one of them was bound to hit. As for *Looking for Kitty*, I had given up on that one. The finished movie would live on a shelf with all those unproduced screenplays.

A few weeks later, I was more than pleasantly surprised when my agents called with unexpected news. They seemed to have a buyer for *Looking for Kitty*. Mark Urman of ThinkFilm liked the movie and wanted to talk. Mark had cofounded the distribution company in 2001 and was heading its theatrical division.

"He does have some notes. Would you be willing to sit down, hear him out, and maybe make some of the changes? If so, I think they'll buy it."

"What do they want to pay?" I asked.

"Nothing," he said.

"Nothing?"

"Nothing."

"It's a partnership," he explained. "What's called a no-advance partnership."

In short, this meant they were going to buy the movie from us for nothing. They would distribute it, in this case worldwide, and after they broke even on costs, we would split the profits fifty-fifty, or whatever percentage we negotiated. With nothing better on the table and the film on my shelf, I thought why not, and soon Aaron and I were meeting with Mark Urman.

Mark's notes on *Looking for Kitty* were similar to the thoughts Aaron and I had shared after watching it. The film felt like two different movies. One is a more melancholy story about this private detective who is mired in another era, and the other is a buddy comedy with some goofy situations. Mark wanted to see more focus on the PI. He thought this was the stronger story.

We made the changes with existing footage and also ran outside and shot a couple extra scenes, the benefit of shooting digital. We brought in several editors and got the film to a place where it finally seemed finished—or as finished as we could get it. I know *Looking for*

Selma Blair and Patrick Wilson in Washington Square Park on *Purple Violets*

Kitty should probably have never seen the light of day. To me, it still feels like the B-side in a rarities album, but it accomplishes nothing on the shelf.

WHAT TO DO WITH *PURPLE VIOLETS*

Now I was faced with the challenge of selling *Purple Violets,* the best of my most recent films and maybe one of the best I had ever made. The marketplace for independent films was in flux. A number of specialized distribution companies like Paramount Classics and Fine Line had closed their doors in October 2005. So it was no surprise when we premiered *Purple Violets* at the Tribeca Film Festival and

Going over a scene with Debra Messing on the set of *Purple Violets*

were not met with a bidding war afterward. There were no seven-figure offers. Instead, we were offered another "no-advance partnership," which was becoming the new standard offer for specialized film distribution companies. Aaron and I agreed we were not doing that again. Fortunately, our financing producer, Pam Murphy, also wanted to explore other options. There had to be another way to reach our audience, we thought.

SELLING IS ONLY PART OF THE STORY

It was a less than advantageous position to be in at the time, to say the least, and I had no idea things would get even tougher over the next few years. At the end of the day, I had to figure out a strategy for my situation in that moment. In a way, I was back to square one. I have heard novelists say that every book is like starting over. Movies are the same way. Each one requires you to start the whole process from the beginning.

One day, a few months after we failed to find a distributor for *Purple Violets*, I was walking from the Village to my apartment, and I found myself thinking about my *McMullen* experience. What had made it buzz-worthy?

I realized that when selling a film to the public, especially a small independent film, you not only need to sell the story, actors, and genre, but you also need a couple other related stories around the film to generate press. The movie was only part of the narrative. With *McMullen*, Fox's PR team identified a few such stories. One story was that it was Fox Searchlight's first movie. The new, artsy offshoot of the big studio was written up in all the major business sections across the country, and *McMullen* was mentioned in each one.

There was also the story of the twenty-seven-year-old former *Entertainment Tonight* production assistant who lived in his car for a time and who made a feature-length movie at his parents' house, which starred a bunch of no-name kids from New York, and hey, it was pretty good. It also took home the Grand Jury Prize at the Sundance Film Festival. A studio's marketing and PR team can do a lot with all that, and they did.

As I recalled the stories we had pushing *McMullen*, I realized I needed a story about *Purple Violets*, something more than going on a talk show and explaining why I made the movie. There was no story in our releasing this movie in New York and LA in a typical distribution platform, as we did *The Groomsmen*. We'd just be ignored again.

I found our story one night when I was home looking for something to watch on iTunes, which had only recently premiered their movie and TV store. I noticed that episodes of *Sex in the City* and *Grey's Anatomy* were the two most popular shows being downloaded. I realized that the audience who loved those two shows might also love *Purple Violets*, a movie about a thirtysomething female novelist and her best friend dealing with these two guys they liked in college. That's when it hit me. The audience for *Purple Violets* wasn't headed to the art house on a Tuesday night; they were home in their living room looking for something to watch on iTunes.

Through a friend, Adam Rackoff, who worked at Apple, we were put in touch with Glenn Bulycz, the senior manager of iTunes movies. We pitched the idea to Glenn about premiering *Purple Violets* exclusively on iTunes. He was excited, especially with the idea that iTunes would be the only place to watch/download *Purple Violets*. Based on the company's enthusiasm, I knew we had our second story.

Together with the executives at Apple, we discussed the various ways we could distinguish the film in the marketplace and create buzz around the film's release. In addition to the banners that would appear on both the iTunes home page and the iTunes movie page (which we recognized as prime real estate), the trailer would play at many of the flagship stores across the country in their screening rooms. We also worked with Apple's publicity department to send out iPod touches, with the movie already downloaded, to key journalists.

The iTunes movie page was only a year old at that point (the service became available in September 2006) and had only about 500 titles on their site. Now they have over 65,000. Apple had never premiered a film on iTunes, and they were excited to see if the experiment would work. If we were a success, there would be no question that other independent films would follow, looking for viable alternatives for distribution.

Still, I was nervous. This had never been done before and I was a filmmaker. I wanted to see my film projected on the big screen in a darkened theater. That was the dream. The dream was not to have someone watch it on their computer or their phone. Then I thought back to my days at film school when I first saw *The Godfather* or *Taxi Driver* or *The French Connection*. I didn't see those movies in a theater. I saw them on VHS tape on a twelve-inch television screen. And in pan in scan! I loved those movies anyway. Was it the ideal way to see them? No. Did I love them any less? No. I thought to myself, beggars can't be choosers. I need eyeballs. I need to get my film in front of an audience that wants to see it, and I was pretty sure I had found that audience. But still, was this really what we should be doing with our movie?

Before agreeing to the deal, I sought advice from my friend in the music business. Record stores were long gone; buying and discovering music online had become the new norm. When I told him about the pending arrangement, he said, "Apple? iTunes? You're crazy not to get in. It's the future."

Aaron and I were sold, and again, we were lucky Pam Murphy thought out of the box like us. She was as excited as we were to embrace the future.

That was it. We got in.

FOR SALE ON iTUNES

The process turned out to be similar to a traditional release. The digital window simply replaced the theatrical window. After two months of exclusivity, the movie would be available in whatever ancillary markets we could exploit (including, in our case, the DVD release with the Weinstein Company as well as pay cable with Showtime, basic cable with Lifetime, and foreign sales).

The biggest difference was availability and accessibility. For most of my films, I and the actors in my cast were recognizable enough that we could get on the national talk shows and promote a movie the weekend it opened in New York and Los Angeles. It would take another two or three weeks for the movie to expand into Chicago, San Francisco, and Denver, and by then the promotion would have been forgotten.

As for people in markets like St. Louis or Columbus, they might have to wait two or three months before the movie would get to their local art houses, if it got there at all. By releasing the movie on iTunes, anyone hearing about my new film could download the movie immediately. You want to watch? Just click. We were doing something novel by releasing a movie exclusively on iTunes. We knew we were onto something.

The *New York Times* called pretty quickly after we announced the deal. We ended up on the front page of the *New York Times* Arts section, as well as the cover of weekly *Variety*. We received coverage on NPR and in *Moviemaker* magazine. The *Los Angeles Times*, in an editorial piece on October 29, 2007, wrote:

> With most of the major Hollywood studios spurning the iTunes store, Apple may be eager to use "Purple Violets" to show the industry how powerful a partner it can be. The potential here is for Apple or another player with a direct line to consumers—say, Netflix or Amazon.com—to become a more efficient and profitable way for filmmakers to find an audience, just as Starbucks and Wal-Mart have become the independent distributor of choice for established acts such as Paul McCartney and the Eagles.
>
> One problem for Apple is that its downloadable movies cannot be burned onto conventional DVDs, making it harder to watch them on a living-room TV. Although solutions are emerging, the market just may not be ready for what Burns is doing. Still, it's good to see someone taking the risk.

Our plan was working. We were not only a movie story, but we were a business story. The movie was generating far more press and publicity than it ever would have received had we accepted the no-advance partnership offer and opened up in the traditional art house structure.

Of course, there were still skeptics out there who questioned the strategy. I remember a few snarky film journalists asking if I thought someone would ever watch a movie on their computer. One guy pulled out his phone and said, "Do you really think someone will ever watch on a screen like this?"

I had the movie downloaded on my phone. I picked it up off the table and pushed PLAY. We watched for a moment.

"You know what?" I said. "This image is better than ninety percent of the VHS films I watched in college on a twelve-inch color TV. So, yeah, I think people are going to watch it."

Purple Violets was released in mid-November 2007. Though major newspapers didn't review the movie, users did, and that was more than enough to make this first digital release a success. In the second week of availability, the film ranked number two out of five hundred available titles, behind only *Pirates of the Caribbean*. More people saw it than would have with a traditional release. And we made money. Our investor took home a sizable six-figure number from iTunes, more than she would have if the film had opened in New York and LA and then disappeared.

After our two-month deal with iTunes was up, we licensed the film to the Weinstein Company. Now it's one of those movies, along with *McMullen* and *She's the One*, that is licensed year after year, all over the world.

In the end, *Purple Violets* found an audience. People saw the movie, and that's all I wanted.

FOURTEEN

TIME TO CHANGE THINGS UP

I n 2008, on top of the recession, the indie movie business was in major flux. Mark Gill, the former president of both Miramax Films and Warner Independent, confirmed as much when he gave his famous "The Sky Really Is Falling" speech at the LA Film Festival in 2008. Speaking in front of the finance group, Gill described getting a call from a director friend who asked how he was doing. "How good can I be?" he replied. "I work in independent film."

Gill understood the laughter that followed came from a painful place. He outlined the reasons for his answer, listing major production companies that had closed or cut their staff, the financiers who had split the scene, the glut of movies and dearth of theaters, the costs of promoting a movie, and competition from video games.

"Here's how bad the odds are: Of the five thousand films submitted to Sundance each year—generally with budgets under ten million dollars, maybe five [make money]. That's one-tenth of one percent. Put another way, if you decide to make a movie budgeted under ten million dollars on your own tomorrow, you have a ninety-nine-point-nine-percent chance of failure.

"If you want to survive in this brutal climate," Gill continued, "you're going to have to work a lot harder, be a lot smarter, know a lot more, move a lot faster, sell a lot better, pay attention to the data, be a little nicer (okay, a lot nicer), trust your gut, read everything, and never, ever give up."

When I read Gill's speech that spring, he was telling folks what Aaron and I had known. Making indies has always been hard, and finding success with those films even harder . . . but now it seemed impossible.

I had been in the business thirteen years, I had written and directed eight movies, and I was barely making a living. I knew I needed to change things up and I needed to make some money. I made a commitment to myself that the next script I wrote would be something I could do with a studio and a bigger budget. I wanted to tell a story against a large canvas with a lot less dialogue and a lot more action.

Additionally, I called my agents and told them, maybe more realistically begged them, to find me an acting job. I spent the next few years acting in the films *One Missed Call* and *27 Dresses* while trying to write that studio movie. In that time, I wrote four screenplays: *Rainy Dog*, a turn-of-the-century crime story based on a 1997 Japanese film of the same name; *No Sleep Till Brooklyn*, a *Get Shorty*–esque ensemble crime comedy; *Fresh Kills*, a buddy-cop action film; and *Man for the City*, a political thriller I cowrote with my good friend Rob Port.

We attempted to get each one of these films made, with the

exception of *Fresh Kills*. As I had tried with *On the Job* and *Legs*, we went out to a number of high-profile movie stars but couldn't get one of the big names attached. What was wrong?

When looking back at those years and those scripts, you might wonder if I would have been more successful had I been more patient. Instead of writing four screenplays over the course of two or three years, maybe I should have taken that time to write just one. Is that what it takes to write a great screenplay? Quite honestly, I don't think so. I'm not a lazy writer. It's not like I banged out one draft in a month and then sent it on its way. When you write every day, you get a lot done, and I did numerous drafts on the three scripts we sent out. I was even introduced to the great screenwriter William Goldman during those years, and he offered notes and assistance on the final drafts of *Man for the City*. He thought it was terrific and was surprised when we didn't attract a star for the lead.

As I said earlier, I write every day because I enjoy it. I never find misery in it. Each one of these screenplays was a joy to write. Goldman put it best: "It's about going into a room alone and doing it." To me, writing is about banging out a first draft and then fixing it. The only secret about good writing is the need to rewrite. You have to do it. Goldman's Tenth Commandment of writing is "Thou shalt rewrite." For some writers, solitude is also a necessity. But sometimes, the quiet room isn't an option. Sometimes, you're on the subway or a plane or sitting in a coffee shop and inspiration hits. I've made it a habit to get those thoughts down then and there. Sometimes, it's just a line of dialogue. Sometimes, it's twenty pages. Again, if you're overprecious about the process, the harder it is to get the work done. And you'll find once you get started, the time at the keyboard flies by.

I would show up each morning in my writing room, where I'd have chalkboards, dry-erase boards, and corkboards covered with scene ideas, lines of dialogue, and character descriptions. I hung photographs and paintings that reminded me of the mood and the tone I was trying to create. I'd make a big pot of coffee, sit down at my computer, and jump in. It was and still is the best part of my workday.

I look forward to disappearing into the story and interacting with the characters I've created. Even when I'm working off an outline, I enjoy surrendering to where those characters take me. That's always the best part of the writing process: when something appears on the page in front of you that you didn't anticipate or labor over, and it makes you laugh or smile or it even shocks you. You have no idea where the notion even came from. All you know is that it's good and if you weren't sitting at the keyboard at that exact moment, it never would have come to you. You disappear into the world you've created. And that's where the fun starts. You become steeped in the characters and their problems; and few things are as interesting as figuring out what happens to them. It can be a lot more fun than your day-to-day life.

Larry McMurtry wrote the novels on which two of my all-time favorite films were based, *Hud* and *The Last Picture Show*, and he most recently won an Oscar in screenwriting for *Brokeback Mountain* (which he shared with Diana Ossana). Larry describes screenwriting as "far from being hard work, and might actually be considered to be a form of creative play." It is. Which is why I keep doing it in spite of all this rejection I'm sharing with you.

However, reflecting on those three screenplays, maybe I should have been more patient during the submission process. I knew from past experiences that if you're not making a fully financed studio movie, in which a significant payday is involved, your script tends to be treated as a low priority for the movie stars you're pursuing, and for their representatives. In other words, to get that bigger budget, you need a movie star attached, but without a fully financed movie, many movie stars won't read your script. It's a classic catch-22.

On each one of those three scripts, we made an offer or two to big-name movie stars, knowing that it usually takes a minimum of four weeks to get a response and, in some cases, can take six months to get read. As you may be realizing, I'm not built to wait six months for anything. As Woody Allen famously described in *Annie Hall*, "A relationship is like a shark. It has to constantly move forward or it dies. I think what we have on our hands is a dead shark." I'm very much like that when it comes to my projects. Once I stop writing, and we start trying to put together a cast, the waiting for me begins to feel like a slow death. This period is typical for any movie, but when a month or two goes by and there is no forward progress on the project because we are awaiting an actor to read the script, I get very agitated if I'm not distracted by something else.

Therefore, the minute we made a submission to one of these movie stars, I knew I'd have some time on my hands. That's when I would begin the next screenplay. In some cases, by the time we finally heard back from the actor and they passed on the project, I had already finished the first draft of my next script. Maybe my problem was that I fall in love with the script I am currently working on. This makes it much easier to move off the previous script and throw all my energy into a new project.

Perhaps this wasn't the best strategy, because three years went by and not only did we not get any of those movies made, we never even got close. Part of the problem lay in the fact that the movies had much bigger budgets (each was budgeted at $25 million or more). There is a small pool of actors to draw from when you're looking for that much money.

However, by quickly moving off a project and onto the next one, I felt like at least I was giving myself a fighting chance. I know too many filmmakers and writers who, upon finishing their most recent script, spend all of their time in the "putting the project together" phase (nagging agents to read the script, having meetings with producers, hustling financiers, etc.). As I said, this process is usually comprised of torturous waiting. A year or two can go by, and while all this effort is directed at trying to get the movie made, no new material is being generated.

The big, unfortunate takeaway here is this: For every movie that gets made with a movie star, there are thousands of good screenplays by talented writers that never see the light of day. As I said before, filmmaking isn't easy, but that's not why we do it. We do it because it chose us. We didn't choose it. Besides, what's the alternative?

Aaron has reminded me on numerous occasions that we need to always have several irons in the fire, and we should pivot quickly to the project that is getting traction. Given how tough the movie business is, we never believed in having all of our eggs in one basket.

So in the spring of 2008, while we were still hoping to attach a movie star to *No Sleep Till Brooklyn*, I read about the Red One, a new digital camera that Steven Soderbergh had recently used to shoot *Che*. Soderbergh stated, "This is the camera I've been waiting for my whole career. Jaw-dropping imagery, recorded on board a camera light enough to hold in one hand." I immediately called Will Rexer and asked him to meet me for a drink. We met at Puffy's Tavern in Tribeca, where we would later shoot a number of scenes in *Nice Guy Johnny*, and over a couple of beers, I picked his brain about the Red. Will had shot on the Red many times for commercial shoots, and he, too, was a fan. Given the cost, I suggested we split the bill and buy one together. (It retailed for a relatively inexpensive $27,000, with extras costing another $5,000. By comparison, a high-end 35 mm film camera was well over six figures.)

Will knew he'd be able to rent it out on any commercial shoot he was doing, and I thought it might give us an opportunity to play. As disappointed as I was by the *Looking for Kitty* digital experiment, I did enjoy the freedom that the smaller camera afforded us. You could really run-and-gun. When we received our Red that summer, I was anxious to get out and shoot something. Rather than go out and do a typical camera test, I suggested we make a short film.

During this time, I was already busy on my next feature-length screenplay. Still convinced I needed to make a more mainstream movie with action elements, I came up with the idea for *The Lynch Pin*. The hero of this screenplay, Dan Lynch, is a poor man's Jason Bourne—a half-assed hit man in a Calvin Klein suit who was looking to get out of the business but had *one more job*. I would never get around to finishing that screenplay, but I pulled a scene from the script in which Dan Lynch is being pursued by a rival hit man through crowded New York City streets. For our short, Will and I decided to replicate the handheld jittery camera movement that Paul Greengrass had employed in his *Bourne* films. However, we'd have just a two-man crew. Also, one of the guys in the crew would also be playing the lead role of Dan Lynch.

Will threw the camera on his shoulder and we walked a few blocks up from Tribeca to Canal Street, where an actor I had called, Dara Coleman, agreed to meet us. I played Lynch, Dara played the rival, and three hours later we had our foot chase in the can. No permits, no lights, no sound, no wardrobe, no hair, no makeup, no nothing. Then we ran back to my office, downloaded the footage onto our editing system, and watched. We were blown away. This did not look like digital. The game had changed.

I had fallen in love with this camera. But more important, I was reminded of something else I love—getting out and shooting. I quickly pulled the plug on *No Sleep Till Brooklyn* and tossed yet another script onto the shelf. I then extracted about twenty-five minutes' worth of scenes from *The Lynch Pin* screenplay and reworked it into a short film.

Over the course of the summer, Will and I called in a number of favors both from actors we knew and from a handful of good friends to play the parts of Dan Lynch's victims, including Aaron's wife, Brigette. Because the camera was so small and versatile, we took it with us wherever we went. When Will and I attended Aaron's wedding in Los Angeles, we made sure we shot a few scenes out there. When P. T. Walkley had a concert in New Orleans, we followed him there to shoot a few more scenes. In addition to Canal Street, we shot all over Manhattan, including Times Square at five in the morning; Central Park, where we assassinated our former editor, Thom Zimny; and in various hotel rooms.

Shooting *The Lynch Pin* that summer was just what I needed. It had been several years since I was behind the camera and in the editing room. And I missed it.

We didn't feel this was the kind of short film that you would submit to a film festival. So we weren't quite sure what to do with it. We thought maybe we would just throw it up online. That's when we came up with the idea of cutting it down into three-minute episodes and turning it into a web series.

And that's what we did. Here's the link:

https://www.youtube.com/watch?v=FJDfa6xrEuI

DIRECTOR FOR HIRE

Here's the problem with a web series. Especially one made back in 2009. Or at least the one we made. There was no way to monetize it. And like anybody with two kids and a mortgage, I needed money. So it was about this time that my agents suggested I forget about being an indie filmmaker once and for all.

"Why don't you think about directing something for the studios," they said. "Let's see if we can get you a director-for-hire job."

This was not a new discussion. I had been approached in the past about my interest in directing romantic comedies for the studios, but I had always said no. I had always just wanted to make my own movies. But things were different now. I needed to make some money. In the past, I could fall back on my acting career when my bills were overdue. The only acting I had done lately was a few guest appearances on *Entourage,* and I got that gig because my brother, Brian, had been a writer on the show.

"Why not?" I said, with a sigh of resignation. "Let's look at some scripts."

Several scripts were sent my way. None of them made me jump out of my chair and say, "I have to do this," but I did read one romantic comedy that was pretty good. It was funny and it seemed like it could be a hit.

I called my team.

"Let's meet with them and see," I said.

"Great," they said. "Let me call the studio and set it up."

"You know, it's Thursday afternoon," I said. "Do me a favor. Let me sit with it over the weekend. I'll reread the script and if I feel the same way on Monday, let's go ahead with the meeting. I just want to give it a little more thought."

I spent all weekend thinking about what it would mean to say yes, what I might gain versus what I would give up. I had spent my entire career building a personal and identifiable body of work. I wanted to continue making those kinds of movies, one a year, in New York City. Maybe break it up occasionally with a cool cop movie or a badass gangster film. That was all I really aspired to do. I had a pretty good run at it, too. My first film worked, and I kept making movies. Granted, each one got increasingly harder, but I felt if I directed a studio movie, especially this romantic comedy, I would be conceding defeat. All the credibility I had built up by sticking to my guns, by being true to my initial dream—being the guy who made those small, talky New York movies—would be lost. I would lose all that currency in and out of the business—and with myself.

On Monday morning, I called my agents and broke the news.

"I'm sorry," I said. "The script is good, but it isn't for me. I can't do it."

FIFTEEN

HOW THE HELL DID THIS HAPPEN?

I had failed to get any of my big-budget crime films going—all the way back to *On the Job*—but it was still the genre I wanted to explore. I knew part of the reason I hadn't been able to get any of those films made was because people didn't believe I could pull it off. I knew if I was ever going to break out, I would need to make the movie that showed them I could do it.

So I decided I would try, yet again, to make an Irish American gangster movie. That script was *Stoolie*, the story of a low-level criminal who returns home for his father's funeral to discover that the neighborhood gangsters think he's the guy who dropped the dime on them and sent some of their friends to jail. The plot was not unlike *Ash Wednesday*, but this time around, the characters were real, the dialogue felt honest, and I wrote the script with the budget in mind.

I gave it a contemporary setting. I was done trying to get a period movie made and I didn't want to limit where I could shoot like I had on *Ash Wednesday*. I wanted to make it down and dirty. We'd shoot it on our new favorite camera, the Red One. Handheld. Immediate. Intimate. In your face.

The script went out to our agents and immediately got some good buzz. We were happy we didn't have to chase another elusive movie star and we quickly assembled a cast of well-respected actors, which included David Morse, Dermot Mulroney, Ali Larter, Jennifer Esposito, and me. All signed on, knowing they would be paid peanuts.

Nothing excites an actor more than the opportunity to play a character who speaks, thinks, and feels like an actual living, breathing person. Unfortunately, the parts available to most actors these days are thankless, one-dimensional characters whose sole purpose is to service the plot of studio programmers in the comedy, action, and horror genres. And admittedly, I've played my fair share of these cardboard cutouts. (Perhaps you've seen my stellar work in *One Missed Call*.) That said, when you commit to these films, you know what you're getting into—you're not there to sink your teeth into a meaty role and show the world what kind of chops you have. However, they do tend to pay the bills. And it's tough to knock that, especially these days.

But sometimes you've got to ignore the money and get back to why you got into this business to begin with. In most cases, you got bit after seeing something like Nicholson in *Chinatown* or Pacino in *Dog Day Afternoon*. I've yet to meet an actor, writer, or director who decided to get into the movie business after hearing how much Schwarzenegger got paid to do *Kindergarten Cop*. You wanted to be part of something that might live on after you, something iconic, something memorable.

Which is why there are quite a few actors out there who are

willing to work for almost no pay, especially when they are given the opportunity to disappear into a good part. It's why actors love to do theater; it's why, in recent years, big names are showing up all over cable television shows; and it's why indie film will never die.

Aaron and I budgeted *Stoolie* at $2 million. We thought for sure with this cast it wouldn't be a problem. Wrong again.

Despite the ease with which we assembled our actors, and the enthusiasm they and their agents had for the material, the financing was an altogether different story. There was no shortage of people who liked the script and a few people were circling. But again, there was resistance to me as a guy who could make a crime film.

Despite the attention for innovating with iTunes, I wasn't coming off the kind of success that would give me latitude to stray beyond my sweet spot.

There were still a few places considering *Stoolie*, but as we've learned over the years, the longer the deliberation, the far more likely their decision will be to pass. Almost every movie I have done has happened within a couple weeks from when we've submitted the material. We would send the script on a Friday to financiers and within weeks be in negotiations. It had now been several months, and hope was dwindling. Aaron and I knew at this point that *Stoolie* was probably dead. We'd have to call our actors and let them know that we would be pushing the project, which meant we weren't making the film any time soon. After *Legs, Rainy Dog, No Sleep Till Brooklyn,* and *Man for the City,* not being able to get this film financed hit especially hard. We thought we did everything right on this one. Nonetheless, it appeared as if another script would be going up on the shelf.

Then, we got a call that a financier was a fan of my films, liked the script, and wanted to meet. Aaron and I met at his office. We weren't dead yet. Ideally, this financier would respond to my vision of the film, give us the $2 million we needed, and then we'd shake hands and go off and make the movie. That was wishful thinking.

We were informed by my agents that while the financier liked the script, he had significant notes. There was nothing unusual about this, as the person footing the bill has a lot of leverage and will ask, if not demand, conditions be met—whether it's using their crew, casting a friend, or pushing the material to their liking.

Even so, our meeting had just started and already I wanted to get the hell out of there. The notes were not ideas that supported my vision of the film, which was a drama with crime elements. Instead, he wanted to push the film into clear genre territory with a lot more action, blood, and gore. I tried to digest his thoughts, while knowing this didn't feel right.

He then brought in his two production guys, who started telling us about their film equipment and production experience, and offering guidance about how to make independent films. Clearly, they would be part of a financing package, and though they were nice guys, we didn't need them. At this point, I had directed eight feature films with budgets ranging from $25,000 to $6 million. Regardless of how many films their production team had made, there was nothing they were going to tell me that I didn't already know. I sat there in shock. These LA guys clearly knew my work and they still had the audacity to tell me how to make a low-budget indie movie in New York City.

To top it all off, as the meeting was breaking up, even though in my mind it had ended within the first five minutes, the financier brought in a young woman whom he thought might be perfect for one of the female leads. At that point, I was done.

Did I really need to compromise this much to get a $2 million movie made? I thought if I was going to compromise, it would be on the bigger studio job, and that made sense. I would be getting paid to direct someone else's script. However, at $2 million, the entire budget would be on-screen, and we would not be getting much at all. The reason you say yes is because you want your movie to get made at all costs. I hadn't made a movie in several years. Do I just swallow the conditions or negotiate them down and surrender to this new reality? Maybe I had to. I was at this point in my career.

When I'm writing, I live with complete conviction that the script I am working on will be made into a movie my way, with actors of my choosing, and the resources I need to execute my vision. However, I know full well when I take it out into the marketplace, I have to confront the realities of the business, for example, meeting with people who have their own vision of the movie, their own casting ideas, and their own methods of making and realizing movies. I know I have to do this, but at what cost?

Aaron and I walked out of the office playing our cards close to the vest. It was one of those assaulting bright days in Los Angeles that did nothing to brighten my mood. We rode back to my hotel, both of us genuinely rattled. Our careers were in real trouble. Aaron and I had a good ten-year run together. We made a lot of movies and we made a little money. Maybe we had reached the end of the line. A change might do us good.

We drove in silence and then started speaking about our efforts those last couple of years. We tried to change up our story realm and budgets, writing stories about cops and gangsters, trying to attach movie stars. And after that pursuit, we learned that maybe the scope of our world was too big. So we scaled down the world while still retaining the guns, sex, and violence, and wrote a script that we could budget at $2 million, which we thought would secure us the financing. We had put together a terrific cast, yet there was virtually no interest in this project. The only nibble we got would be a version that required some major compromise. How had I gone from winning at Sundance with *McMullen*, standing next to Steven Spielberg in Deauville, and costarring with Dustin Hoffman and Robert De Niro to standing in an office, hat in hand, and listening to these B movie producers tell me how to make my movie? How the hell did this happen? Where was the mistake? Where was the fuckup? I've had some doozies but this was a new low.

I was scared shitless about my future as a filmmaker—or apparent lack of one.

The problem came down to money. Orson Welles implied as much when he spoke of having wasted the greater part of his life trying to raise money in order to make his movies and not spending enough of his time actually making films. As he said, "It's about two percent moviemaking and ninety-eight percent hustling. It's no way to spend a life."

I realized I was in the same boat. With the exception of *The Lynch Pin* experiment, I hadn't directed a movie since I was on the set of *Purple Violets* almost four years earlier. Now it seemed as if I wouldn't be directing anything in the near future. So much for one movie a year.

In spite of the challenges we were facing, I knew moving forward on *Stoolie* with a compromised vision was not the solution. I had already made that movie; it was called *Ash Wednesday*.

SIXTEEN

NICE GUY JOHNNY

A aron and I got back to the hotel, had a drink at the bar, and started to reflect on what it was like to be that young guy who made *McMullen*. I was broke back then, I had no experience, no relationships in the business, I certainly didn't own any equipment, and if I wanted to make a movie, I needed to shoot on film and edit in a proper editing bay. And yet, I did it. I made a movie. As I have said, those were the best twelve days of my life.

An idea started to form. Maybe we have a lot more freedom than we think. Maybe those twelve days are sitting right in front us and we're overthinking this whole thing.

You can take all the writing and filmmaking classes in the world, but what you can't be taught is what I knew instinctively and had suddenly rediscovered. If you want to make a movie, if writing, directing, or simply making things is in your DNA, if that's what you plan to do with your life, then you have to do it.

You have to figure out a way to make your movie. I pictured my dad talking to me in the bar after everyone and his brother had rejected *McMullen*.

He said, "Look, if this is what you want to do with your life, if you have to make movies, we'll find a way to get you another twelve days."

The difference between then and now is that I owned the Red One camera. I had a Final Cut editing system in my office, I had a decade of experience making films, and a group of smart people, including Aaron Lubin, Will Rexer, Mike Harrop, P. T. Walkley, and Janet Gaynor, who would all love to collaborate on a project. I certainly knew we would have no problem finding actors, both known and unknown, to work with us.

I told Aaron, "Let's go make a movie and we will apply the same disciplines I did on *McMullen*."

So we wrote down a list of guidelines to work off, eventually calling them the McMullen 2.0 Rules. As with *The Brothers McMullen*, we would self-finance a feature film for $25,000. This number would be our shooting costs, meaning we would get the film shot (or "in the can," as we used to say) for $25,000. Postproduction would eventually cost another $100,000.

We would shoot no more than twelve days.

We would use a three- to five-man crew.

All locations had to be secured for free.

We would hire unknown actors who would be willing to wear their own clothes and do their own hair and makeup.

We would shoot available light anywhere we could. If we needed to light a scene, we would use the absolute minimum, no more than three or four lights, similar to the lighting package that your local news crew might use.

After we had established the rules, we set out to write a script that would work with these limitations. We first thought about the theme of the screenplay. Usually, you don't start a script thinking theme first. Instead, you are crafting plot and story and as you write each successive draft, a theme emerges, as if your subconscious is slowly revealing itself. However, we were at a turning point and looking for meaning in this next project and its subject matter.

Aaron and I talked about how close I was to giving up on my dreams, conceding defeat, and signing on to be a director for hire on a studio movie. We then realized that recently, most of our friends were having to make the same sort of tough decisions. The actors, musicians, writers, and even a few professionals were suddenly being asked to question and sometimes surrender their dreams as our economy continued its downturn.

That's when the initial thematic idea of *Nice Guy Johnny* was born. It would be a story about a guy who is being asked to give up his dream, and we'd explore what that does to a person and what that could potentially cost him.

Having recently gone through my temptation with the studio world, I decided to go back and look at the movies that had turned me on to filmmaking back in film school. I wanted to revisit the films and stories that inspired my dreams in the first place. Here's a few: Antonioni's *L'Avventura*, De Sica's *Terminal Station*, Truffaut's *The Man Who Loved Women*, Rohmer's *My Night at Maud's*, Godard's *Contempt*, Bergman's *Smiles of a Summer Night*, Scorsese's *Alice Doesn't Live Here Anymore*, Cassavetes's *Husbands*, Spike Lee's *She's Gotta Have It*, and a lot of Woody.

I had forgotten what small and personal films these giants had made. These were intimate character studies told with humor, honesty, compassion, and pathos. I was looking for inspiration and I found it. I was recommitted to telling smaller stories and making personal films. Fortunately for me, and any of you who want to make your own movies, these types of films don't require a big budget. Right now, with the cameras available to us, the technology, the fact that everything is better, easier, and cheaper today than it was fifteen years ago, the resources are available for virtually any budding film-maker to go out and make a movie.

McMULLEN 2.0

The next thing Aaron and I did was make a list of the locations we knew we could get for free. The first location we put on our list was my parents' house. A few years after *The Brothers McMullen*, my parents had sold my childhood home, the house where we shot *McMullen*, and moved to Rockville Centre, Long Island. Aaron and I both joked that shooting a few scenes in the new house might bring us good luck. We also put my sister's house on the list, which was also on Long Island. We then listed three other friends' homes on the east end of Long Island where we thought we might be able to call in a favor.

That led to another idea. If we were to shoot the film in the fall, on the east end of Long Island (the Hamptons), the crowds would be long gone, the beaches would be empty, and we could probably get away without having any permits. Given it would be the off-season, we knew we'd also be able to find very inexpensive housing for our cast. That's when we decided that a big part of this screenplay would take place in the Hamptons.

Now we had our theme. We had our setting. All we needed was our story. I had an idea for a character who was nice to a fault, a guy who couldn't say no, the poor schlub who puts everyone else's wishes before his own. That's how *Nice Guy Johnny* was born. We also came up with the idea that our nice-guy hero was a sports radio DJ, a plot point that was a holdover from the *Mothers and Sons* script.

For the next couple of days in LA, Aaron and I started to beat out the story. We had to figure out what his dream was and why he was being asked to give it up. I used the weekend I had spent a couple of months earlier, debating whether to sign on to direct a romantic comedy for a studio, as inspiration. I was a guy who was very close to giving up his dream. I had been very close to taking a paycheck to direct something I was not passionate about. I knew I had to put that into the script.

"He's got to have the weekend I had. The weekend of soul-searching when he has to decide whether he's ready to walk away from the dream."

I also thought about where I was in my mid-twenties. The start of your journey is a much more critical time. At the time I set out to make *McMullen*, people were questioning me. "You're going to write? Direct? Act? You don't know what the fuck you're doing. You don't have any money. Why don't you get a real job?"

I heard all those things.

Imagine if I had listened to them and not gone for it. I would be living a very different life.

That was going to be Johnny. He had to be the guy confronted by naysayers, the guy who had to decide whether to give it up or hang tight.

As for my character, I wanted to create something of a Falstaff, the seemingly idiotic fool who ends up offering sage advice. Not a mentor so much as someone who had lived life, perhaps screwed up, made the wrong choices, but had done it on his terms and, as such, acquired some insight into what was what. If Johnny was a nice kid who thought of others before himself, my character, Johnny's uncle Terry, had to be a grown-up rascal who thought only of himself—a one-way Charlie. Over the course of the film, he gives what sounds like the worst advice to his nephew, but in the end we discover he may actually have known what the hell he was talking about.

SAY UNCLE

I spent the next month back in New York, writing the script. On the first day I sat down at my desk, a lyric from Bruce Springsteen's classic song "Jungleland" popped into my head: "Barefoot girl sitting on the hood of a Dodge/Drinking warm beer in the soft summer rain."

The image of that girl had been with me since I was a teenager. I have always romanticized her and wondered about her. Who is she? What promise does she hold? If my hero Johnny met her in that parking lot, where would his life go? Could she fix it? Was she that catalyst who said, "Hey, man, your life doesn't need to be this. It can be *this*"?

Once I had that, everything about the story fell into place. Johnny Rizzo, an aspiring sports radio talk-show host, had made a deal with his fiancée that if he wasn't making X amount of money by a certain time, he would give up the dream, return to New York, and take a job with her father's friend's corrugated cardboard company. Well, that time has come. He arrives in New York on a Friday, has a job interview on Monday, but already knows he has made a terrible mistake.

To escape his soon-to-be in-laws, he ducks into his uncle's bar for a drink. Sensing he needs way more than a drink, his uncle takes him to the Hamptons for the weekend to talk sense into him or at least have one last run at fun before he walks down the aisle.

At the end of June, with the first draft written, I called our casting directors, Laura Rosenthal and Maribeth Fox, and told them about the project. We told them we wanted to cast unknowns, fresh faces.

"Help me find the kids who keep knocking on the door but lose out on the part because they're not a name yet, kids in their twenties who would be excited to have a break, who were as hungry as Connie Britton was when we made *McMullen*."

One of the first actors we saw was Anna Wood, a dark-haired actress with attitude and range, and we immediately fell in love with her for the part of Claire, Johnny's fiancée.

The following week we saw Kerry Bishé, a lithe blonde with all the qualities of the girl I imagined Bruce singing about in "Jungleland." She seemed perfect for the role of Brooke, the winsome girl of summer who inspires Johnny to think about what his life could be if he follows his passion rather than the promise he made to his fiancée. Eight seconds into her audition we all agreed, "That girl is a movie star." We cast her as Brooke, and we knew then that our instinct was right about casting the unknown kids. There are a ton of talented actors out there, just waiting for the break and eager for the chance to sink their teeth into a good part. Our casting directors had done it again.

Finding the right guy for Johnny wasn't as easy. We needed an actor who was immediately empathetic on-screen. We finally found those qualities in Matt Bush, an actor who had done a couple of TV pilots but had an energy and likability that made Aaron and me ask the same question: How come this kid hasn't been discovered yet? The same was true for all these kids. That's one of the perks about shooting in New York. We have an enormous wealth of undiscovered actors to draw from.

6 DAYS, 67 PAGES

From day one of shooting, this young cast showed up prepared, ready to work, and determined to prove themselves. This was their moment. I quickly realized I had to up my game. In the scenes Matt and I had together, he came at me with everything he had. They all did. Whether we shot eight or nine pages a day, these kids always knew their lines. If anyone flubbed a line, it was always me.

We shot our first six days in Manhattan and at my sister's and parents' houses on Long Island over the course of a few weeks. Just as we did on *McMullen*, we worked around our paying gigs, finding a day here or there when we were all available and could get together and shoot. We knew the bulk of the shooting would take place in early September out in the Hamptons, when we would all move out there for a week and shoot the majority of the screenplay. Our six days in the city were a good warm-up, a chance to work out the kinks. It gave our tiny crew a chance to figure out how we were going to pull this off. We had an ambitious schedule and workload ahead of us. We were going to try and shoot nearly seventy pages in six days.

The movie gods were smiling on us when we arrived in the Hamptons. The weather was astonishingly beautiful. The beaches—some of the world's most gorgeous—were empty.

We worked eighteen-hour days and shot sixty-seven pages that week. By comparison, a good day on a Hollywood movie, you'll finish two or three pages of the script. We did quadruple that amount with a minuscule crew, not the typical army you go into production with. We joked that we were more like a five-man Navy SEAL team. Among Will, Aaron, and me, we had forty-five years of indie film-making experience. We knew what we needed and what we didn't need. We knew where to spend what little money we had and we knew what not to waste our time on. We had been doing this a long time and it was paying off.

Will obviously took care of the lighting and camera work. Mike Harrop (now our line producer) handled sound. Nick Newbold was brought in as a jack-of-all-trades and did everything: lugging gear, assisting Will with lighting, boom operating, and driving the vehicles. He also proved to be a grill master, cooking up burgers, steaks, and fish on the BBQ. Aaron's wife, Brigette, was brought on to help with wardrobe and also made sure there was plenty of beer and wine at the end of the day.

By day two, we were cranking. For a two-page sequence that culminated with Johnny and Brooke meeting at the beach, we probably did fifteen setups in one hour, racing against the setting sun. On a normal film, something like that would take a full day. Every time you move the camera, everyone and everything behind the camera—the whole army that comprises a movie crew—has to move, too. We didn't have the big machine to slow us down.

Will just grabbed the camera and we knocked off one take of the wide establishing shot. We then quickly marched the camera forward and grabbed two takes of our medium two shots. Then we marched a little closer and grabbed two more takes of our over-the-shoulder shots, and then closer still, for two takes of the actors' respective close-ups. In under an hour the scene was done, but with a little bit of light left in the sky, Will wasn't ready to stop yet. He threw the camera over his shoulder, and he and Nick marched twenty yards out into Gardiners Bay to grab one last wide shot with the perfect magic-hour glow. I look at that scene now and can't believe that's how we shot it. The rule book says that's not how it's supposed to be done. It was a frenetic, energizing, and exciting way to make a movie.

At the end of day twelve, during our last dinner together at Rowdy Hall on Main Street in East Hampton, I looked around at my bare-bones crew, all of whom had spent the last six days sweating and fighting and grunting it out for me with no promise of a paycheck. Everyone had a smile on their face (and a beer in their hand), and I realized then that this crew I had put together was less a film crew and more an indie rock band. We were like that struggling five-piece that gets together, writes songs, rehearses, records, and then hits the road, with no promise of anything other than getting a chance to do what they love and the hope that their collective effort will pay off. No financier cut the check to support their cause and therefore they don't have to make any compromises. And that's what we did, too. None of us expected to make a dime off this project. We all wanted to do something that we could feel proud of. We raised our glasses many times that night and cheered our good fortune. Twelve days of it.

Back in New York, we set up an editing station in my office. The technology had changed considerably since the last time we made a

Making a movie for $25,000—on the set of *Nice Guy Johnny* on Long Island

feature film. Instead of needing to rent an Avid editing system and a costly editing suite, we purchased the Final Cut editing software from Apple and downloaded it onto a desktop computer.

We knew that postproduction has certain costs—including sound work, color timing, title creation, and sound mixing—that are necessary to absorb, and it is the most expensive part of making microbudget films. Fortunately, Mike Harrop was an expert in this arena and figured out ways to make it even cheaper for us. Ultimately, our postproduction budget was about $50,000. If you're keeping score, we're only in the hole $75,000 at this point.

Even with that low number, we knew we couldn't afford to hire a seasoned editor. We had to find someone as hungry as our actors were. Aaron and I both immediately thought of Sarah Flack's assistant, Janet Gaynor. We had been very impressed with her work ethic when we worked with her years before, and she had done a great job cutting a dream sequence in *Looking for Kitty*. Mike Harrop had stayed in touch with Janet and gave her a call. Was she ready to make the leap? She jumped at the chance to be our editor. Needless to say, she rose to the occasion and did a great job cutting the film. She has been our editor ever since.

OPENING IN 40 MILLION HOMES

The world of film was in a state of rapid change. In 2000, Netflix took on video rental giant Blockbuster, mailing movies on DVD to 300,000 subscribers. In 2010, Netflix now boasted more than 20 million subscribers and streamed movies on the Internet; and the once mighty Blockbuster was in bankruptcy. The theatrical movie business was still strong, but theaters were making the bulk of their money on Hollywood blockbusters. Attendance for indie or specialized movies—movies that opened on 300 screens or fewer—was down. According to *The Wall Street Journal*, independent studios saw their share of revenue decline to 19 percent in 2010, from 33 percent in 2001.

In April 2010, we screened *Nice Guy Johnny* at the Tribeca Film Festival, which was becoming a home court for us. I had been involved with the festival since day one, when festival founders Robert De Niro and Jane Rosenthal asked me to help launch their effort. Jane and Bob founded the festival to celebrate New York City as a major filmmaking center and to contribute to the long-term recovery of Lower Manhattan after the attacks of 9/11.

Given that I was a Tribeca resident, I jumped at the chance to get involved, and since that first festival, I have been lucky enough to premiere six of my films in front of my hometown crowd. There is no better audience for a New York filmmaker than a packed house at the Tribeca Film Festival.

The premiere of *Nice Guy Johnny* was no exception. That night, our three young unknown actors, Kerry Bishé, Matt Bush, and Anna Wood, walked the red carpet and posed for photographs with Robert De Niro. Had nothing else happened with the film after that night, our little movie would have already been a huge success in our eyes.

Fortunately, a lot more success was to come *Johnny*'s way. We knew we had a great relationship with Apple after debuting *Purple Violets* on iTunes in 2007. Given what that film made, we thought if we released *Nice Guy Johnny* exclusively on iTunes and did half the business that *Purple Violets* did, we would still turn a tidy profit.

After that first screening, we got some interest from a number of indie distribution companies. Yet we knew that our best chance to make money on this film would be to forgo a theatrical release. We knew where our audience was. They were at home watching their favorite TV shows and movies on their flat-screen television sets. According to *The Economist*, the share of Americans who attend a cinema at least once a month declined from 30 percent in 2000 to 10 percent in 2010. It was then that my lawyer, John Sloss, suggested we complement our iTunes strategy by adding Video-On-Demand as a major component of our release plan.

John made the argument that instead of a theatrical release, where we would open up in two theaters, one in New York and one in LA, we could now open up in 40 million living rooms—basically the entire country—on the same night. Then it would be available for a couple of months. Cable television and, more specifically, On-Demand were underexploited and undermonetized. With the exception of Magnolia Pictures, which had experimented with a handful of movies that were released on VOD prior to their theatrical run, few other filmmakers and distribution companies had looked at VOD as a viable release platform.

"The other advantage is you'll also retain ownership. All we do is license the movie," he said. "The movie is your child. You nurtured it, created it, and understand it like no one else. The notion of then handing it over for twenty years to someone who has nowhere near the emotional connection and who has twelve more movies waiting behind it is, to say the least, counterintuitive."

I got it. But this was an enormous gamble. Unlike Magnolia's films, we would be forgoing a theatrical release altogether and fully embracing this new distribution platform as our primary form of distribution. Like our gamble with *Purple Violets*, we felt that betting on new media and changing viewer habits was the way to go.

There was another advantage to this game plan. As I had seen with *Purple Violets* and *McMullen*, every movie needs a story about the movie, something that gets it noticed, and thanks to John Sloss, I had mine. Instead of Video-On-Demand being the backup plan, it turned into the game plan. We would not make excuses for our non-theatrical release. We would embrace it.

I knew this idea would work because I had heard from fans of mine over the years that they often missed my movies because there were no art house theaters near where they lived. For example, the last time moviegoers in St. Louis got to see a film of mine play in their hometown theater was probably ten years ago. Our releases never reached that platform. If they did eventually make it to some of the secondary markets, it was usually too late. When the actors and I did press for the release of earlier films, we would go on the talk shows, do the radio interviews, and sit down for all the magazines and newspapers to build awareness. But if you didn't live in LA or New York, by the time the film got to your town, if it even did, odds were you had forgotten about the movie. This was less of a concern in 1995, but in 2010, filmmakers were trying desperately to compete for a slice of a rapidly dividing pie. We were no longer competing just with network television as we had seventeen years earlier. We now had to compete with everything that came with the Internet: Netflix, Hulu, Facebook, Twitter, etc. This in addition to the fact that a big percentage of our audience now preferred watching at home.

John argued that we wouldn't have to compete if we went with a digital VOD release. He said when I did publicity for the movie, whether it was the *Today* show or Jimmy Fallon, I could inform people that if they wanted to see the movie, they could pick up their remote, switch over to their On-Demand channel, and watch it immediately. And that's what I did.

In October, *Nice Guy Johnny* was released—or became available— on Comcast, TimeWarner, and Cox cable systems, among other places, as well as on iTunes.

I realized I could also have a theatrical release. It was called the festival circuit. Instead of the film playing on a tiny screen in a small art theater, in each one of these cities, we played in their best movie house. We knew that hitting the festival circuit would help build buzz and hopefully positive word of mouth throughout the independent film community. We screened the film for various festivals and film societies in Chicago, New York, Austin, Woodstock, Fort Lauderdale, San Francisco, Savannah, Boston, and Washington, DC, where we found crowded theaters and receptive audiences, people who were seeking out this kind of film. They became influencers and they did the legwork. I did Q&As at every stop, and before leaving, I would say, "Tell your friends they can see the movie On-Demand or on iTunes tonight!" And it worked.

At one point during the film's release, *Nice Guy Johnny* cracked the top 20 on the iTunes rental chart. I then took to Twitter and asked my followers to help spread the word and see if we could move the title into the top 10. After two days, the *Nice Guy Johnny* army was able to influence enough folks out there to push *Johnny* to the number 6 spot. There was only one other independent movie in the top 20 with us—the indie hit *Winter's Bone,* which was nominated for four Oscars, including a nomination for Jennifer Lawrence in the Best Actress category.

Twitter would become increasingly important to me over the next few years. I had first started using the social networking service about a year earlier when Ted Hope suggested that I engage with my audience. He said that indie filmmakers need to find five hundred true fans (he later changed it to five thousand true fans) and engage with them in a meaningful way, and they could then act as your influencers. He said I should open myself up to them and start a dialogue.

I was reminded of my film school days, when I was walking up Sixth Avenue about twenty feet behind Spike Lee. I wanted to go up to Spike and ask him one hundred questions about how he had made *She's Gotta Have It*, but instead I respected his privacy. I then thought Twitter might give me the opportunity to answer some questions that a kid in film school might have for me. I took to Twitter immediately and found the correspondence with my fans rewarding. (But more on that later.)

It wasn't just Twitter that helped turn *Nice Guy Johnny* into a financial success. The great challenge we had with our digital release was

Producer Aaron Lubin wearing many hats on *Nice Guy Johnny*, with Kerry Bishé and Matt Bush

financing the marketing and publicity of the film ourselves, since we weren't working with a distribution company. We budgeted $40,000 for publicity, taking our total budget to $125,000. The $40,000 paid for our PR company but left nothing for marketing costs. As a result, in addition to using social media, I would have to go out and do as much publicity for this film as I could, which meant talking to anyone who would listen.

I hit it off with publicist Sean Cassidy the second I met him. He's an Irish New Yorker with an affinity for *The Brothers McMullen*. He was also a guy who handled press for major brands like Delta Air Lines. He didn't usually represent actors or filmmakers, but he was excited about the idea of working together. He thought that *Nice Guy Johnny* would be a great opportunity to sell the movie and rebrand me as a filmmaker who was continuing to pioneer low-budget ways of making movies. He was instrumental in getting the message out for McMullen 2.0. With his help, I spoke to dozens of newspapers, magazines, radio DJs, and talk-show hosts to get the word out there. We also benefited from the fact that the biggest cable provider, Comcast, had a relationship not only with Sean but also with our friends at the Tribeca Film Festival. We sat down with the Comcast folks in Philadelphia, and they explained that they saw On-Demand as a new place for indie cinema. Their idea was to drive traffic toward all of these wonderful indie films that they had on their shelf. They wanted On-Demand to become a destination for indie film lovers. This was music to our ears. They launched the Comcast's Indie Film Club, which became a curator for independent cinema, helping Comcast's vast audience find these films. I worked to help promote the club and *Nice Guy Johnny*'s association with it. This provided great exposure for the film and helped turn *Johnny* into a financial success.

We were also introduced to indie film consultant Marc Schiller, who runs a company called Bond Strategy and Influence, which has a nontraditional, entrepreneurial approach to marketing an independent film. Marc and his team target tech bloggers, hip websites, tastemakers, and connectors to help create buzz on films lacking bigger marketing budgets and resources. This approach worked hand in hand with our digital distribution model. And like an entrepreneur, Marc agreed to work on the film for a percentage of the profits. Now, every year, we send him a check.

We simply did everything we could do for free to get the word out there. We even cut a series of trailers to look like trailers for classic foreign films like Antonioni's *L'Avventura* and Bertolucci's *Contempt*, which we called, "homage trailers," with the hope to gain further buzz. I had now learned that if you want to be an indie filmmaker, you have to be as creative in the release as you are in the making of the film.

I had simply gone back to the basics and made a movie the way I had fifteen years earlier, with no money and no names. Along the way, I learned a lesson in resourcefulness. The business had changed, and I had to change with it if I wanted to keep making movies—and making them on my terms.

Now it looked as if I would be able to do just that. As we began to see the numbers, I realized we were probably going to make a nice profit, and money would keep coming in each quarter. No one got rich, but we made a movie with no outside interference and the movie turned a profit. It's important to remember that you're not going to become a millionaire doing this. But that was never the point. Over the years, I think a lot of people in the indie film business kind of took their eye off that. Everyone got disappointed if their movie didn't do $10–20 million. You know, we're the equivalent of the indie band. We're not supposed to sell out Madison Square Garden. You're supposed to see us at the Bowery Ballroom and say, "Oh, that was a killer, great small show."

For us the metric is not winning the theatrical box office for the weekend but, rather, charting on some of these new distribution platforms. And given *Nice Guy Johnny*'s success on iTunes as well as On-Demand, I didn't have to think about what to do next. My next move was obvious: I was going to make another movie.

t took me fifteen-plus years to relearn what I had done instinctively
on my first film. Back then, I was motivated by desire and necessity. All these years later, nothing had changed.

The journey had been a lesson in filmmaking, my independent
education. It had returned me to my roots—only smarter and wiser.
With *Nice Guy Johnny*, I didn't need to go hat in hand, begging someone
to give me a couple of bucks to make a movie, then have to listen to
their notes, and finally to look for distribution. I proved I could make
a movie, distribute it, and make some money.

It was about this time that I compiled what I called my two lists
of compromises. In one column, I listed the things I would have to
do without if I made a microbudget movie:

—I will not be working with movie stars.

—My camera department will have no toys (i.e., cranes, car rigs, Steadicams, dolly track, etc.).

—I will not get paid and neither will my crew.

—I will not work with a production designer or costume designer or location scout or script supervisor or hair and makeup departments (you get the idea).

—My movie will have no stunts.

—There will be no giant set pieces.

—No art can be created for the film.

—No transportation will be provided for the actors.

—There will be no trailers.

—There will be no money for locations, so we will need to beg friends and family.

—I will have no special effects.

—I will need to lug equipment and move furniture when needed.

—We will not have permits, so we will have to steal shots where we can.

—We will eat pizza most days for lunch.

In the other column, when someone writes you a check, the list of compromises includes:

—You will no longer have creative control.

—You will not be able to cast the people you want to cast.

—You may have to change your title.

—You may have to change your music.

—You may have to make changes to the screenplay that you do not agree with.

—You may have to hire crew members you don't care for.

—You may have to cast someone's girlfriend.

Now when I sit down to write a screenplay, I pull out my lists of compromises and decide which list I want to use. But if you're like me, and you're okay telling smaller character stories, then it's obvious which list I prefer to embrace.

Armed with a blueprint, I jumped straight into the next film, *Newlyweds*. While promoting *Nice Guy Johnny*, an idea began to percolate. I wanted to do another pseudodoc as a companion piece to *Sidewalks of New York*. Aaron and I had long talked about a sequel. I also wanted to do something for the upcoming tenth anniversary of the Tribeca Film Festival, given my long history with them. I thought maybe a film that would be a love letter to Tribeca itself.

Those notions came together one night when Christy and I were at a dinner party for a couple's tenth wedding anniversary. While toasting his wife, the guy said, "After ten years, if this thing wrapped up tonight, I think you could call it a big success." After we all laughed about the sad reality of that notion, we got into a conversation about what makes a marriage successful in this day and age, and that inspired my screenplay.

Initially, I thought about examining marriage at different stages through three couples. The first was a couple on their second marriage. Pragmatic, they felt like "All right, we screwed up the first time, we're older and wiser now, and we'll make this work." The second couple were empty-nesters whose marriage was dissolving. And the third couple was breaking up after just getting engaged.

During the writing process, though, I fell in love with the first couple, the character I intended to play, Buzzy, and his wife, Katie. I also fell out of love with the third story. What emerged was a snapshot of a couple, newly married for the second time, whose pragmatic bliss is disrupted when the guy's half sister brings her crumbling hot-mess-of-a-self to their house. I was intrigued by the idea of truth and honesty in relationships, the question of what we choose to share with each other and how the little white lies people tell one another can pile up and take a heavy toll. I spoke to real couples who said that it wasn't the big, catastrophic events like an infidelity that broke them up. More times than not, it was the little, petty things that piled on top of each other over the years.

As I mentioned before, I like to go into investigative mode when writing about relationships. I ask friends and family their views on whatever subject matter it is I'm exploring. When writing *Newlyweds*, I went on Twitter to cast a wider net. I asked my followers about the first big fight they had with their spouse after they were married. What put an end to the honeymoon period? Almost all of them told a story of some family member, whether it was a mother-in-law or brother or cousin, who had stirred the pot somehow. This information sent me on my way to creating the primary plot in the film. The two newlyweds would each have a family member who would drive a wedge between our heroes.

This is the first and only film where we did not rely heavily on a casting director. As I wrote the script, I was writing with certain actors in mind. I conceived the part of Linda for Kerry Bishé, who had just blown all of us away in *Nice Guy Johnny*. I also wrote parts for two other *Nice Guy Johnny* cast members, Max Baker (whom I first met when acting in *Life or Something Like It*) and Marsha Dietlein (who had actually auditioned for the Jennifer Aniston part in *She's the One*). Caitlin FitzGerald had auditioned for us on another project and I knew she was perfect to play the female lead, Katie. While writing the script, I was also acting in the film *Man on a Ledge* and became friends with one of my costars, Johnny Solo, and cast him in the role of Miles. The last part was cast after Nick Newbold turned us onto his friend Daniella Pineda's YouTube comedy sketches. We thought she had the right combination of sass and humor that we were looking for, and cast her without an audition.

I wanted this film to be "a total collaboration" with my actors. I met with them while writing the script and asked them for their input. I wanted each one of them to have the opportunity to play the kind of character they thought best suited their acting strengths.

We also decided to change from the Red One to the Canon 5D, an even smaller and less expensive camera. I wanted to make it easy to run downstairs and shoot with just a few minutes' notice. Will Rexer heard it was being used for commercials. We looked it up online, jumped on a subway, got to the camera store, and bought one for $2,800.

Then, as I said in an interview with the *Chicago Tribune*, "I put a sweatsuit on and called my friend who owns a gym and said, 'Hey, we need to come in for a half hour and do a camera test.'"

There, we shot one-half of my character's phone conversation (which ended up in the film). We went back to my office and looked at the footage and it was great. Will looked at me and said, "I guess we're making this movie." The Canon 5D's size—or lack of it—made the camera conducive to shooting out on the street or in a restaurant or a coffee shop. Most of the scenes took place in those types of locations. Without lights. Without sound. We didn't get permits or permission. People looked at us for a minute or two but then lost interest. So smaller was easier. It removed yet another layer of complication. Simply, we were free to pick up the camera and shoot whenever we felt the urge. One morning when I was taking my kids to school, the snow started to fall. Anyone who has been in New York during a snowstorm knows how beautiful the city can look when those giant flakes are falling from the sky. I wanted to take advantage of that and shoot something, but Will wasn't available that day. The great thing about making a movie on the 5D is that even a novice photographer can capture a pretty great image, especially shooting daytime exteriors. We called Kerry Bishé to see if she was available to shoot a quick scene before the snow stopped falling. She jumped on the train and hurried down to Tribeca. We quickly rehearsed the scene where she runs into my character outside on the street. I framed the shot, handed the camera to Nick Newbold, our jack-of-all-trades, and we began shooting. Nick ended up doing such a great job that day that we used him later in the production to grab some additional pickup shots.

We shot the film in fifteen days over the course of three months. This gave me the opportunity to have several weeks in the editing room between shooting days. I was able to use that time to look at my footage and performances and rewrite according to what I liked or what wasn't working. I've equated it to a painter looking at his first wash and then being able to sit back and look at his canvas for weeks before deciding what brushstrokes to apply next. This is a luxury of time that a filmmaker is rarely afforded. Typically on any movie set, the minute the check is signed and money is being spent, it is a mad dash to the finish line.

This is understandable, but it can also make for a frantic environment on set. There is usually someone standing behind the filmmaker, reminding him that he needs to "make the day." If the filmmakers don't make their day, they go over schedule and then over budget, which is obviously a legitimate concern for money people.

We never had to make the day with *Newlyweds*. We were just out on the streets of Tribeca with a tiny handheld camera, and on some days with just a two-man crew, having a good time and hopefully doing good work.

When we finished shooting, our total production budget came in at $9,000, which was $2,000 for insurance, about $5,000 for actor salaries, and the rest for food, travel, and other smaller expenses. After postproduction and PR expenses, *Newlyweds* cost about

$125,000—still a fraction of what was considered to be a low-budget movie.

TRIBECA

While editing the film, I received a call from my friend Nancy Schafer, the executive director of the Tribeca Film Festival, asking if our film would be ready for the festival's tenth anniversary. A short time later, Nancy and Geoff Gilmore, the festival's creative director, came to our cutting room and watched a rough cut. They loved it and all the local scenery and right there scheduled it as the closing-night film. Talk about a well-spent $9,000.

While preparing for Tribeca, we started to think about a poster for the film. I had been giving my Twitter followers a day-by-day report on the progress of the film, and I could tell they were appreciative of the access. I then thought it would be cool to give someone in the Twitterverse an opportunity to design the movie's poster. I tweeted the idea to my followers and was met with great enthusiasm.

We then launched a movie poster design contest from my website and received close to a hundred entries. We asked folks to vote on their favorite, and the winner was David Ayllon, who was invited to join us at the festival's closing-night screening of the film and the party afterward.

We had so much fun with that contest that we also launched a song contest. Songs were submitted and of the fifty-plus entries, I chose Patrick McCormack's "Ovenbird" to play under one of the scenes in the film. Patrick joined David at the closing-night festivities in Tribeca.

The closing-night screening of *Newlyweds* was one of the best screenings I've ever had. It was on par with that first screening of *The Brothers McMullen* at Sundance. We were playing in front of a hometown crowd and they got every joke and nuance. There's nothing like sitting in a packed house and hearing the laughs in all the right places and raucous applause when the film ends. It was my tenth film as a writer-director-actor and I felt I had finally resurrected my career.

In December 2011, we licensed *Newlyweds* to Tribeca Film, the festival's new distribution arm. They released the movie on VOD, iTunes, Amazon, and new platforms like Vudu (a content delivery service). Instead of opening in two theaters, we opened *Newlyweds* in 45 million homes—as we did with *Nice Guy Johnny*.

Newlyweds turned out to be far more profitable than we ever could have imagined. In addition to outgrossing *Nice Guy Johnny* on both its VOD and iTunes release, the film brought a very solid fee when John Sloss licensed it to Netflix. Because we had almost no marketing costs, high distribution fees, or manufacturing expenses, for example, film prints and DVDs, the film moved into the black within a few weeks after its release. Our little $9,000 film had turned into a genuine moneymaker for us, and we continue to see profits come in every year.

There is no greater feeling than when your faith is rewarded. And when you can reward the faith that people put in you. After we re-couped the $125,000 investment we made in *Newlyweds*, we were able to cut back-end checks to our crew. This team was with our project for months, going from preproduction to the film's release. They worked tirelessly on the sheer hope that the film would be

As low budget as you can go—shooting *Newlyweds* on the Canon 5D

profitable. We were able to give checks that would exceed their rates on other independent films, in some cases by multiples of two or three.

SUPERSERVE YOUR NICHE

It was now summer 2011. *Newlyweds* had already played at Tribeca and the deals were done for On-Demand later in the year. I had booked the summer with back-to-back acting projects, a new HBO pilot, *40*—Doug Ellin's follow-up to *Entourage* that didn't get picked up—and *Alex Cross*. Rob Cohen was directing the reboot of the Alex Cross franchise created by novelist James Patterson. Tyler Perry was cast as Alex Cross, and Matthew Fox was cast as the bad guy. I was cast to play Cross's childhood best friend and partner in the Detroit Police Department.

Tyler and I had a lot to talk about, being two writer-director-actors, and we bonded immediately. One day, we were having lunch together, and he had just rewatched *The Brothers McMullen*.

"What do you think ever became of those McMullen guys? Why didn't you ever make a sequel?" he asked.

I didn't have an answer. Truthfully, I had never thought about it. The movie was a hit. Afterward, there had been talk of developing it into a TV series, which I wasn't interested in. Until that conversation with Tyler, I had never thought about writing the next chapter. There were too many other stories I wanted to write.

He said, "*McMullen* is your most critically acclaimed film and *She's the One* is your most successful. They're both about Irish families." In fifteen years, I had never gone back to the well.

Tyler said, "You have an audience waiting for you to tell stories about Irish Americans. Take some advice from me; you need to su-perserve your niche. That's what I do and if you do the same thing, I guarantee your fans—all those people who loved *The Brothers McMullen*—will thank you for it."

After lunch, I walked back into my trailer, opened my laptop, and wrote:

INT. FITZGERALD KITCHEN—DAY

I had no idea what this script was going to be. I only knew that it was time to return to the Irish American working-class milieu of my first two films.

EIGHTEEN

THE FITZGERALD FAMILY CHRISTMAS

The initial idea that sparked was to write something about a big Irish American family. I grew up surrounded by these types of big families. Two of my best friends were one of nine, and one of eleven siblings, respectively. Both of them always spoke about how their families were broken down into subsets or mini families. For example: the three older siblings, the three middle siblings, and the three youngest had very different relationships and thoughts about their parents. Sometimes, given their age differences, they barely knew one another. Or in some cases, the older siblings actually raised the youngest kids in the family. As a writer, I was most interested in exploring the idea that although kids can grow up under the same roof with the same parents, as adults they can have very different opinions on who their parents are and what kind of job they did raising them.

In this screenplay, I imagined a deadbeat father who had bailed on his kids years earlier, looking to return home to make amends. The older siblings don't really have an ax to grind with their father, as he was home for much of their childhood. But the youngest siblings despise him because when he walked out on their mother, they were still little kids. I was looking for a device to try and get all of these adult siblings under one roof. I also needed a plausible reason why so many things might be coming to a head for these characters, and that's how I settled on writing a Christmas story. Typically around the holidays, there can be a lot of pressure when any family gets together, even just the pressure for everyone to get along. It's also a time when people make big announcements, such as they're having a child, getting separated, getting married, etc. So the idea to have the film take place during Christmas would be a great device to satisfy those two elements.

I knew I didn't want to make the sappy, goofy, funny Christmas comedy. My favorite Christmas film has always been *It's a Wonderful Life*, another film that has the perfect blend of light and dark, comedy and drama. George Bailey has to cover a lot of tough ground to get to that payoff. I also wanted my characters to go on a tough journey so that when the Fitzgerald family got together in the end, it felt earned. As I started to work on the screenplay, a theme of forgiveness started to present itself. Given that it's one of the themes of Christmas, it tied together nicely.

The script poured out of me and within four weeks, I had a first draft. I had been sitting on these types of characters and their voices for a long time and they were clearly ready to get out. I never had to stop and think: Who were these people? Where did they live? How did they think? Where did they drink? What did their homes look like? Or any other intimate details. I knew these people because I literally grew up with them.

By the time we wrapped *Alex Cross*, I had completed the first draft of *The Fitzgerald Family Christmas*. It brought me back to familiar territory—to family relationships, to the drama that takes place in kitchens and backyards, to Long Island, and to working with my *McMullen* cohorts Connie Britton and Mike McGlone.

BEGGING AND BORROWING

I knew this film needed to feel authentic. I was returning not only to the Irish American working-class milieu, but I was also returning to Long Island. As we started to scout locations, I wanted to find family homes that felt real. Everything from the look of the kitchens, living rooms, and bedrooms to all the tchotchkes. As I pictured the film in my head, I imagined the Fitzgerald family living in my childhood home, but there were two reasons we couldn't shoot there. First, the McMullen clan had already claimed that as their set, and as I mentioned, my parents had sold the house.

I still wanted the Fitzgeralds' home to feel like the houses in my old neighborhood. So I called my mother and asked her if any of her friends still living in Valley Stream might be willing to let us shoot in their house. She called her friends, Tina and Tom Costello, who immediately agreed. It was an odd feeling shooting the final Christmas dinner scene in the Costellos' dining room and having flashbacks to my childhood, where I had dinner at virtually that same table.

I also called friends of mine on Long Island, describing the types of homes I envisioned, and we were able to find real lived-in locations. My good friend Tom Pecora proved to be an invaluable resource. We ended up shooting in his mother-in-law's house, his sister's house, and one of his childhood best friend's homes.

Anytime I write a script, I always think about environment. While we were scouting locations on Long Island, I started to snap photographs of people on the street to inform how my characters would dress. I ran into an old friend in the Green Acres Mall. He was wearing a black leather jacket, an Argyle sweater, and a gold chain and crucifix hanging outside the sweater. The minute I saw him, I knew that was the wardrobe my character would wear.

FAMILY REUNION

I knew I wanted to work with Kerry Bishé, Caitlin FitzGerald, Marsha Dietlein, Johnny Solo, and Dara Coleman, all of whom I had just worked with on *Newlyweds*. I was especially excited about the idea of working with Mike McGlone again. I told him about the project while I was writing it and he was eager to join the cast. When Mike read the script, he immediately recommended an actor he had just worked with and thought would be perfect to play the patriarch of the Fitzgerald clan, Ed Lauter. I was a big fan of Ed's work and the fact that he was also from Long Island made my decision to cast him a no-brainer.

At this point, given the film was about a family reunion, I thought, "Why not unite the cast in something of a family reunion as well?" Aaron and I then decided to try and fill out the cast with mostly actors we had worked with before. And that's what we did. We cast Heather Burns (*The Groomsmen*), Anita Gillette (*She's the One*), Nick Sandow (*No Looking Back*), and Connie Britton. Connie did me a huge favor by joining this cast. She was already shooting *Nashville*, and as much as she wanted to play the part of Nora, it looked like it was going to be impossible, given her schedule. However, she said if we could figure out a way to get her in and out in a few days, she would make it work.

We thought it would be fun casting all these actors we had worked with before, but it also gave us another bonus. Since so many of them had known each other for a long time, the minute we started rolling cameras, you could feel the history between these actors. That was something we did not anticipate, and it added another level of enjoyment to the project.

When it was time to promote *The Fitzgerald Family Christmas*, we felt very strongly about focusing on the screenplay and the themes we were exploring. There was so much press that surrounded the $9,000 budget of *Newlyweds* and the return to the *McMullen* model for *Nice Guy Johnny*. So we purposely steered away from all conversations about the budget for *Fitzmas* and the "making of" aspects of the project. However, so many people have asked me what the budget was for *Fitzmas*. Did we abandon our microbudget approach?

I was a juror that January at the Sundance Film Festival, and I was pleased to see that an old friend, Tom Rothman, had joined me on the jury. Rothman mentioned that he had seen *Fitzmas* and said it was my best movie since *McMullen*. I then told him we made it on a low budget and asked him what he thought we had spent. He guessed the budget was in the $4–6 million range. When I told him that the total cost was $250,000, he couldn't believe it.

Since *Fitzmas* was now our third microbudget film, we had mastered the formula and the rules of how to make these movies. And we kept our schedule to fifteen shooting days. Like the first two films, we relied on friends to help identify some locations we could get for free. Since we were such a small crew, and had no plans to move things around, the homeowners were happy to have us.

Almost twenty years after *McMullen*, working with Connie Britton
on *The Fitzgerald Family Christmas*

The four-man crew who made *Nice Guy Johnny, Newlyweds*, and
The Fitzgerald Family Christmas: Gregg Swiatlowski, Mike Harrop, Nicolas Newbold,
and William Rexer on location in East Hampton

Additionally, we asked the actors to again wear their own clothing and apply their own makeup/do their own hair.

The biggest difference with *Fitzmas* was that we had a much larger core group of actors than we did on *Johnny* and *Newlyweds*, and that required a little more planning. On some days, we used two Red cameras and asked a friend of Will's to help us for the day.

We knew the budget would not allow us to move the camera around, though we wanted to give the film a look of high production value and make it beautiful. The solution would require creating elegant compositions and well-choreographed scenes.

We studied the films of Sidney Lumet, who made New York City movies with subdued camera work and beautiful compositions. We specifically looked at *Prince of the City* and its outer-borough interiors, the kitchens, living rooms, and backyards all photographed with restraint and patience.

TORONTO

It had been more than ten years since a film of mine was invited to play at a major film festival like the Toronto International Film Festival, widely known as the most prestigious North American festival and the venue where most Academy Award campaigns start their run. Aaron and I recognized the importance of this moment.

Four years earlier, we had driven in silence back to my hotel in Westwood after digesting that our final shot at getting *Stoolie* made was dashed. We had figured our filmmaking careers were all but dead. And here we were four years later, receiving news that our film would be premiering at Toronto. We knew that the hard work had paid off. Our entire cast and crew flew to Toronto and walked the red carpet. It was as good an experience as you can have as an indie film-maker. The house was packed and the crowd loved the movie. Joe Leydon, in his positive review for *Daily Variety*, said, "Burns' dialogue rings true with its deft balance of blunt-spoken humor and emotionally charged vernacular, and his straightforward directorial approach is eminently suitable to the material."

The following morning, as Aaron and I flew back to New York together, we reflected on the past couple of days. While we were appreciative of the kudos and were happy to be embraced by the indie film community after what felt like a long absence, we both recognized that we didn't feel any different. That's not why we do this. At the risk of sounding like a broken record, we do it because we have no choice. It's who we are.

Given our success with *Newlyweds*, we licensed *Fitzmas* to our friends at Tribeca Film. And two months after Toronto, the film premiered on iTunes, On-Demand, Amazon, and other digital outlets. Tribeca released it in a handful of theaters to ensure reviews by the major newspapers and critics (most top critics do not review films that don't have some form of theatrical release).

The strategy paid off. When the film opened two months later, *New York Times* film critic Stephen Holden wrote a glowing review. This was the first positive review the *Times* had given me since *The Brothers McMullen*.

> This comfortably lived-in movie, written and directed by Edward Burns, offers a textbook example of screenwriting concision. Volumes of information and drama are conveyed with minimal dialogue in a tone so relaxed and offhand you hardly notice the painstaking craftsmanship that went into it. . . . Mr. Burns shuffles

this dense material with the dexterity of a card shark. The pace, although swift, is never rushed. The writing and acting give you vivid enough tastes of the characters—there are seven children, two parents, and assorted spouses, lovers and friends—so that each registers as a singular flavor.

I have to admit, reading that review felt great. I thought *The Fitzgerald Family Christmas* was my best film yet. It felt like the maturation of seventeen years of figuring out how to make movies.

CONSIDER YOURSELF LUCKY

When you get to do what you want to do, consider yourself lucky. At this moment, anyone who dreams of becoming a filmmaker is lucky indeed. For the first time in the history of cinema, filmmaking does not need to be a capitalist enterprise. You no longer need millions of dollars or even thousands of dollars. You are no longer beholden to someone writing a check. It no longer needs to be a business. It can be your artistic expression. When I started with *The Brothers McMullen*, it was nearly impossible to make a movie without real money. Film stock and film processing were expensive. Editing on film was expensive. Finishing on film was expensive. Striking your 35 mm print was expensive. Now you can buy a consumer-model digital camera and the image looks great, unlike the grainy, muddy look of my first film and many of the indies from the eighties and nineties. You can even shoot a pretty good-looking movie on your smartphone and then edit it on your laptop. You can do your color correct and sound mix in your apartment on your desktop computer. To top it all off, you don't have to max out your credit cards and go broke in the process, and you don't have to answer to any financial backers. You can post your film on YouTube, Vimeo, and any number of digital platforms and slowly build your audience. Or you don't have to concern yourself with an audience. You can do it for the simple reason that you have something to say. You can pick up your camera, run out into the street, and play, experiment, and make mistakes. If those first films are terrible, who cares. You're not going to end up hundreds of thousands of dollars in debt. You can make a lot of mistakes because, for the first time, you can afford to. You can learn how to make movies and tell stories by making movies and telling stories. Please don't listen to the naysayers who complain that we have a glut of movies, that there are too many people making films. Has anyone ever complained about too many poems, songs, or paintings? Because of these technological advances, you are now no different from the kids who keep writing songs on their guitars until they figure out what makes a good song, or the painters who keep throwing colors up against the canvas until they realize their vision. Think about that kid from Hibbing, Minnesota, who picked up an acoustic guitar and changed the way we looked at the world. Do you think those songs could have been written if Bob Dylan needed to please a money man? Not very likely. That could be you and your camera. You'll never need to answer to anyone. You can just go out and do it. What did Clint famously ask in *Dirty Harry*? "Do you feel lucky?"

Yeah, I do. But I'd made three microbudget movies in three years. Now it was time to return to bigger-budgeted filmmaking. If nothing else, I wanted craft services, goddamnit.

THE McMULLEN BOYS

Aaron, Will, me, and the rest of the team had fallen in love with making movies again. We had eliminated the stress of trying to get the movie financed and proved we could work whenever I had a script ready. And we had absolute creative control. We had found our audience again and figured out how to make money in this business for the first time in fifteen years. However, we all agreed that we were tired of using our own cars and clothes, asking actors to do their own hair and makeup, and begging friends to let us shoot in their apartments, homes, bars, restaurants, gyms, etc.

I had been thinking about Tyler Perry's advice. "Superserve your niche," he had said. When I took *Fitzmas* out on the festival circuit and to the various film clubs and film society screenings, one thing was obvious: Tyler was right. The audience appreciated the return to my filmmaking roots. Tyler had also asked me what happened to the McMullen boys. Since that conversation, I had been giving it a lot of thought.

The rights for *The Brothers McMullen* would be reverting back to me from Fox Searchlight at the end of the year. Also, the twentieth anniversary of the film's premiere at the Sundance Film Festival was two years away, in January 2015.

Therefore, I concluded that the next thing I should write was the sequel to *McMullen*. I figured I'd spend the next ten months writing the script and, assuming we could raise a few million dollars, then shoot it in the early part of 2014. That way, we'd have the film ready for Sundance 2015.

While making *Fitzmas*, I had spoken to both Mike McGlone and Connie Britton about how fun it would be to revisit those characters. As I mapped the story and character arcs, I found myself losing interest in the group of adults and their marital problems and sexual relationships. Instead, I was much more excited when I was writing the handful of flashbacks that I had worked into the outline. I was cutting back to the young McMullen boys and who they were as children when they all lived under the same roof. I had also introduced the abusive father they refer to in the first film. That's when it hit me. I should be writing the McMullen prequel, not the sequel.

I decided to set the story ten years prior to when we shot McMullen. Set in 1984, the oldest brother, Jack, would be a senior at St. John's University, where he meets his future wife, Molly. My character, Finbar, would be a senior in a Long Island public school, and the youngest brother, Patrick, an eighth grader in a parochial Catholic school. As soon as I came up with this take, it dawned on me that I could kill three birds with one stone. Ever since reading James T. Farrell's *Young Lonigan* of the Studs Lonigan trilogy, I wanted to tell the story of my final days in a Catholic grammar school. And like almost any filmmaker who has seen *American Graffiti*, I, too, wanted to take the quintessential look at my senior year of high school. I also had an idea for a rom-com about a couple, set against their last months in college.

With all of these inspirations, I began to outline the prequel. I tweeted the idea to my followers, and the response was overwhelming. Folks seemed to love it. I then tweeted my two working titles, *The Young McMullens* and *The McMullen Boys*. The voting was too close to call and the title is still up in the air. Writing the script was a walk down memory lane for me. I've always been a nostalgic guy and I was loving every minute of it. Then one day my agents called. They asked me if I was interested in television.

NINETEEN
MOB CITY

t was late summer 2013, and I was on the set of *Mob City*, a six-hour miniseries about LA gangsters, set in 1947. Three-time Oscar nominee Frank Darabont was making it for TNT, and I was playing Bugsy Siegel. Dressed in a 1940s suit, a gun in my hand, and armed with some of the juiciest dialogue an actor could ask for, I was having a blast. Ever since optioning the rights to Bill Kennedy's book *Legs*, I had always wanted to play a gangster. What could be better than playing the womanizing, volatile, Brooklyn-born Siegel? I always love a job that doesn't require me to curb my accent. When my agents called me about the offer, and I knew Frank Darabont was at the helm, I jumped at the chance.

I spent that summer traveling back and forth to LA. I was having fun playing Bugsy and working with an incredible group of actors. In addition, Frank was opening my eyes to the cinematic possibilities of

Bugsy Siegel at work on *Mob City*

TV. The HBO series *Entourage* had introduced me to quality productions, but this was different. TNT had given Frank complete creative freedom and a budget big enough to re-create LA in the 1940s. Essentially, we made a movie every week.

I loved working on the show, and dreaded the inevitable conclusion for Bugsy Siegel, who died in an avalanche of bullets to the face and chest. On my last day, the day Siegel met his demise, TNT's senior vice president of original programming, Lillah McCarthy, was on set talking with Aaron and me between setups.

The daughter of actors (Kevin McCarthy and Augusta Dabney) and a former actress herself, McCarthy said, "It's a shame that you die at the end of this series. We love working with you. Would you ever think about doing television again?"

"Yes," I told her. I had a great time on the show. I also was sorry it was over.

"What about doing more than just acting? What about creating your own show? We're fans of you as a filmmaker as well."

Being fans of shows like *Entourage*, *Louie*, and *Curb Your Enthusiasm*, Aaron and I had discussed the idea of creating a half-hour comedy/drama for cable television several times. I told Lillah as much and mentioned a one-liner dealing with New Yorkers in relationships.

"We're more into cops and gangsters," she said.

I told her I had always wanted to do a period cop movie and had tried to get a number of gangster films made over the years but never thought about trying to do either on television. Then I looked over at Frank, who was standing in the middle of LA gangster Mickey Cohen's office. He had this incredible set built to his specifications. He had three cameras going, an extraordinary cast and crew, and TNT executives who were supportive of his vision. It looked to me like filmmaker heaven.

"Maybe I can come up with either a cop or gangster show," I said.

"If you do, we'd love to hear it!"

The head of the network, Michael Wright, was there later that day and Lillah mentioned our conversation to him. He reiterated their enthusiasm about hearing an idea.

I told him I was heading home to New York for the last two weeks of summer and would give it some thought. If I could come up with an idea for a series, we would set a meeting in September. On the flight home, I was genuinely enthusiastic about the notion, and I knew I needed to spend some real time thinking through what story I wanted to tell. Do I pitch a cop show or an Irish gangster show?

I returned to New York and spent the last days of summer trying to find the idea. Then it hit me. Why not do both? Why not combine the two filmmaking dreams that had escaped me: 1960s cops and Irish gangsters in one show.

I dove back into some of the research I had done on the history of the NYPD and found myself drawn to one particular division of the police department that existed in the mid-sixties. The Public Morals Division was a plainclothes unit of cops that dealt with vice crimes like gambling, prostitution, and after-hours bars. It would be fun to explore their interactions with everyone from high-end gangsters to low-level streetwalkers. The early seventies also saw the end of old-school institutionalized corruption (which dated back a hundred years earlier in New York). I also thought a show that looked at cops in their day-to-day lives and their domestic worlds might be something I could authentically capture, having grown up around cops. Quite simply, it was the perfect world for cable television, and I started to see the endless story possibilities that could be explored.

Moreover, I knew this world could also encompass the Irish gangsters who were involved in gambling, prostitution, and other illegal activity. It was not uncommon at that time for many of these guys, cops and gangsters, to grow up together. One guy might become a cop, and his best friend would end up on the other side of the law. The world was becoming richer.

Both of my dream movie projects, the period cop piece and the Irish gangster saga, could be woven into one seamless world. I was onto something.

As luck would have it, during Labor Day weekend, I was invited to a dinner party in the Hamptons where I saw Steven Spielberg. It had been a while since we had seen each other. As we caught up, I mentioned my experience on *Mob City* and the fact that I was currently developing an idea to pitch TNT. Steven said he was very friendly with the head of programming, Michael Wright, for they had a successful collaboration on *Falling Skies*. He absolutely loved working with Michael and TNT and emphasized how supportive they are to the vision of the creator/showrunner. Steven then asked about the show. I went into detail about the idea, my passion and excitement growing to a crescendo. Steven thought it was a great idea for a show and offered to help.

I had worked with his television team, Darryl Frank and Justin Falvey, several years earlier on a pitch/script about the fashion business for Fox. It was a project Steven brought to me and my wife, who was a model for more than twenty years and knows a thing or two about that world, and we sold the pitch and developed it with Darryl and Justin. Unfortunately, that project, *Ready to Wear*, didn't go beyond the script phase, but we loved working with Darryl and Justin.

My answer, of course, was a resounding yes. Let's do this together.

TWENTY

PUTTING TOGETHER THE PITCH

We set a pitch meeting with TNT for the end of September in Los Angeles. I continued to read a ton of books on the history of the NYPD, both nonfiction and novels. From the first draft of *On the Job*, I had been an NYPD buff, gathering history and stories about New York City from any source I could find. I devoured anything I could get my hands on.

I became especially intrigued by what the police department was like before the Knapp Commission took on corruption in 1972. The Public Morals Division dealt with what they termed victimless crimes—prostitution, numbers, bookmaking, after-hours clubs, and the like. This world was all about the relationships between the cops and the people who ran the gambling rooms and the whorehouses. The line between the good guys and the bad guys was hard to see. They were all city kids. They grew up in Hell's Kitchen, Little Italy, or Yorkville. Some became cops. Some became bookmakers, loan sharks, or numbers guys. They knew one another's families. On Saturday night, they would go to the same bar, forget their differences and talk about the Knicks over beers.

Taking a cue from my two favorite TV series, *The Sopranos* and *Mad Men*, I knew that I needed a single protagonist, a flawed individual who could occupy the center of this male-dominated universe and deal in the gray area between right and wrong. I spent a few days thinking about this guy and the type of character I liked to write. I made notes. Out of that, I came up with Muldoon, a cop who led the division—not by rank but by the strength and influence of his personality.

His personality was enormous, explosive. I drew from my father, my uncle Pat, and my cousin Barry, larger-than-life men who own every room they enter. I liked this guy. He wasn't on track to become a high-level cop or detective. He was content to stay there his entire career as long as the rules he followed were the ones he made. He was a guy who'd found his niche in Public Morals, which I took for the show title.

I wanted Muldoon to be part of a big cop family, like my own, so I added a character to play his younger cousin, Sean O'Bannon, who Muldoon brought into the division and has taken under his wing.

More characters followed. I created a note card for each one and tacked it on my bulletin board. Soon a division took shape, and beyond the division were the cops' families and the neighborhoods where they lived. Then I looked at the nuts-and-bolts architecture of *The Sopranos* and *Mad Men*. How many primary characters did they have? What was the balance between workplace and personal stories?

A framework emerged. I outlined potential scenes and scenarios for the pilot. With an abundance of material created, Aaron and I put together the *Public Morals* bible—a list of characters, backgrounds, and stories we thought fit with them. The notebook was thick. We thumbed through it, adding, shifting, cutting, and pasting.

We did a lot of that in September. All of it was preparation for the pitch to TNT. The pitch would be comprised of the world, the characters, and then the pilot episode. Essentially, I would get in front of them, open the door to this world, and do everything I could to make sure they saw what I did.

Normally, in television, a writer would go in and pitch the show, with the hope that the network would pay for the development of the pilot script. But the story was bursting out of me, and I love writing, and I figured that if they loved the pilot script, they might commit to shooting the pilot sooner rather than later. So I thought, "Why not write the script on spec and hand it to TNT when we pitch the show?" I quietly went to work on the script and in a few weeks I had written a good first draft of the pilot.

Aaron and I got on the phone with Amblin TV executives Justin Falvey and Darryl Frank to discuss our game plan. Darryl and Justin were the same creative, supportive guys that we remembered from *Ready to Wear*. Lubin and I got along well with them and we were all in sync. The only note that raised a cautionary flag came when I revealed that I wanted to add a twist to the pitch.

"We'll go in and pitch it," I said. "But I want to give them a draft of the pilot during the pitch. If I can get the script into good enough shape, and if they bite, I'd like to lay it on the table. 'You like the idea? Here's the pilot.' If possible, I'd like to avoid the potentially long and painful development process. But more than that, I want them to say yes to making the pilot, not to buying the script."

Darryl and Justin liked the idea. I called Steven, and he said the same thing as his TV executives.

"Great," he said. "Send us the script. If it's good, we'll give it to them. If it's not quite there, let's hold off."

"Fair enough," I said.

I sent the script to Steven, Darryl, and Justin. I got their notes and started the rewrite. Fortunately, the pitch with TNT was pushed back a couple of weeks to accommodate everyone's schedule, which gave me a few more weeks to finish the script. I knew these characters, their stories, and all the beats inside and out. Therefore, I was able to turn around a new draft in record time. I sent my rewrite to the group the day before I flew out to LA for the pitch meeting.

I t was a Friday, and the *Public Morals* pitch meeting with TNT was scheduled for three o'clock at Steven Spielberg's Amblin Entertainment office on the Universal Studios lot. My flight into town was easy and I spent the morning at Aaron's house, rehearsing the pitch. We outlined the beats and rehearsed it half a dozen times, to the point where I had it memorized, though not to where my recitation was mechanical. I wanted to keep it fresh, exciting, and conversational. I wanted it to feel like I was telling a story while sitting at the bar with a beer in my hand. I was pretty good at that.

Without traffic, it was a forty-five-minute drive from Aaron's house to Universal. We left an hour and a half early to ensure we weren't late. We did not want to get stuck on the freeway and stress before such an important meeting. Those lessons had been learned ages ago. Note to the neophyte with his or her first big meeting: A successful meeting is about staying cool and focused, maintaining confidence and belief, and being thoroughly prepared. Also, never forget the importance of arriving on time.

Now I was about to pitch them *Public Morals*. And I was parking in front of Steven Spielberg's office, and I couldn't help but flashback to the first time I was there in 1998. I was back at the beginning. A new beginning.

I felt good walking into the meeting. Being at Steven's office gave us the feel of playing on our home court. Heads turned as Michael Wright, Lillah McCarthy, Aaron, and I walked past memorabilia from Steven's films on our way to the conference room, where we were joined by Steven and his two executives, Justin and Darryl. Original Norman Rockwell paintings hung on the wall, as did Rosebud, the sled from Orson Welles's masterpiece *Citizen Kane*—probably the most famous prop in the history of cinema.

The meeting opened with light conversation about *Mob City*. Michael and Lillah said the network was excited about the miniseries, which was scheduled to premiere in early December. They praised my performance and said they were pleased to hear I wanted to act in this show I was about to pitch.

Steven took that as his cue to explain that our project had its origins on *Saving Private Ryan*. His recollection of meeting my dad and uncle and listening to their stories set the stage for me.

When pitching projects, I typically speak for about fifteen minutes, introducing the idea, the characters, and then the story. If I am pitching a TV series as opposed to a movie, I also describe the pilot episode, future episodes, and the overall arc of the first season. At the end, I take questions.

And that's the way I began pitching *Public Morals*. However, three minutes into my description of the world in which the series would be set, Michael interrupted excitedly with the first of several questions. He was locked in, loving the world, and admitting that his mom's maiden name was O'Bannon, the name of our young male co-lead.

The meeting lasted an hour and a half. By the end, I had described all the characters, the pilot episode, and what was going to happen the rest of the season. Everyone talked. Steven served as the best possible color commentator. The energy and excitement was through the roof.

Following a back-and-forth about where I saw the series going over five or six seasons, I mentioned that I had written the pilot and concluded, "I have been sitting on this ever since I wanted to be a filmmaker. I know this world inside and out, I know these people, the cops and the gangsters, and I know this show is going to be fantastic." Michael put down his pen and looked around the table.

"We should do this," he said. "We should definitely do this."

It was then that I pulled out the completed script for the pilot episode and handed it to them. Needless to say, they were surprised. It usually doesn't work like that. They were excited to read the script that weekend and would get back to us on Monday.

Everyone shook hands and dispersed. By any definition, we'd had a great meeting. On Monday, we heard that TNT loved the show and the script and wanted to pick it up.

The pilot was scheduled to shoot in February. We spent the rest of 2013 and the month of January casting the roles and waiting for TNT to deliver a final budget and production schedule. When it arrived, Aaron and I went through the details—along with our line producer, Paul Bernard, whom I had met on *Mob City*—and both of us immediately spotted a figure that put a smile on our faces.

They had given us a shooting schedule of twelve days.

I smiled, enjoying the significance of the number. We were a ten-minute walk from the White Horse Tavern, the bar where my dad had taken me after *McMullen* was rejected by every studio and distributor in the business. All these years later, I could still hear our conversation, like a movie of my own life playing in my head:

INT. WHITE HORSE TAVERN—DAY

Me and my old man sit at a corner table, beers in our hands.

MY FATHER
After you finished shooting your film, you said something to me. Do you remember what you said?

ME
I told you those were the twelve greatest days of my life.

MY FATHER
That's right . . .

ME
And they were.

MY FATHER
Well, did you make this film because you wanted to become rich and famous?

ME
No.

MY FATHER

Did you make the film because you wanted to go out to Hollywood, chase girls, and be an asshole?

ME

No.

MY FATHER

As I recall, you made this film because you had something to say and because this is what you want and need to do with your life. Is that right?

ME

Yeah, that's right.

MY FATHER

Then stop complaining, sit down, and write another screenplay. We'll figure out a way to get you another twenty-five thousand dollars and get you another twelve days. We'll keep grabbing those twelve days every couple of years until this thing does happen for you.

Aaron and I walked to the White Horse that afternoon, sat at the same table, and toasted to another twelve days. After sixteen years, here was my shot to finally make my epic period piece. The best part: I had all those years of experience behind me and a crew who'd supported me through that time. There was no way I was gonna fuck this up.

When I wrote *Public Morals,* I didn't imagine actors in the roles the way I usually do. I pictured the type of men and women I grew up around. All the real New Yorkers. The working class, tough-as-nails, loud and brash, sharp-tongued and sarcastic New Yorkers. I knew I needed to populate the world of *Public Morals* with those folks. This was a tough, working-class environment, and I needed the authenticity of the accents, and the cadence and body language as well, for these types of guys and girls.

It was a no-brainer to engage my longtime casting directors Laura Rosenthal and Maribeth Fox, who have done all of my movies since *She's the One.* As I stated earlier, Laura and Maribeth are the premier New York casting directors and have a tremendous eye for up-and-coming New York talent, as well as for identifying people who work well in my world. We put together the best cast I've ever had the pleasure to work with, including: Michael Rapaport, Wass Stevens, Keith Nobbs, Ruben Santiago-Hudson, Liz Masucci, Katrina Bowden, Brian Wiles, Patrick Murney, Austin Stowell, Lyndon Smith, Robert Knepper, and Tim Hutton. They are tremendous actors, nearly all of them born and bred New Yorkers, and their talent was undeniable. Steven and our team at Amblin and TNT agreed.

PREPRODUCTION

For our crew, Aaron and I wanted to work with the people we had come up with through the ranks. We had spent the last twenty years asking a lot of favors from a lot of people, often asking them to work well below their normal rate, and sometimes even for free. It was time to repay those favors. Our first crew hire was our invaluable director of photography and one of my best friends, William Rexer. We then hired the extremely talented costume designer Cat Thomas, whom I first worked with on *Sidewalks of New York*, followed by several other movies. Cat had gone on to become an A-list costume designer, moving from one studio gig to the next. She worked on everything from Tarantino's *Kill Bill* to, most recently, the Liam Neeson action film *Run All Night*. Cat was family, and in spite of a pay cut, she still wanted to dive into the sixties with us.

Dina Goldman, who was our production designer on *The Groomsmen*, was a keeper as well. Another New Yorker, she was entrusted with re-creating a 1960s New York City. We wanted this to be gritty and authentic, not the polished, staged look some shows are guilty of.

New to our team was Paul Bernard, whom we hired to be the line producer. Paul is also a New Yorker, and I had just worked with him on *Mob City*. He was loved by TNT, which Aaron and I embraced as an advantage, and had experience with a complicated, period production. Paul took great pride in some of the indie films he had produced, and we recognized a kindred spirit. This was a solution-oriented guy. Plus, Paul is a fun person to be around.

We then hired another old friend, Stuart Nicolai, as our location manager. Stuart got his first job on *She's the One*, when he stumbled onto the set of the movie and finagled his first PA job in the movie business, which led to other work with me on subsequent films in the locations department. By 2013, he was a successful location manager in New York and a perfect addition to our New York team.

For our first assistant director, I called T. Sean Ferguson. Sean and I first worked together on *15 Minutes* and I felt he had the right demeanor and old-school personality for the subject matter. This was a guy who grew up in a working-class environment in Manhattan, and had genuine affection and nostalgia for the material.

This prior experience with my crew members gave me the comfort level that was critical, especially given the sheer amount of responsibility I had on my shoulders—writing, directing, acting, and producing. It was important that I could speak in shorthand to the department heads, and not be bogged down learning the rhythms or quirks of someone new. We loved this team, and created an environment where they could contribute and collaborate and where they felt appreciated and respected. Every one of them, without exception, did a fantastic job, and we received loads of compliments about the casting, costume design, production design, locations, and even the scheduling and budgeting.

Now that we had our team, we began preparations for the show. Days were filled with location scouts, casting sessions, and meetings with department heads on the look of the show. Working with the period, I relished the time when Dina and I reviewed countless pictures of New York in the 1960s and strategized with her team about how to re-create it. In particular, I really wanted to harness the grit and clutter and lived-in feel of the police precincts and the Public Morals office. It's hard to fake old, peeling paint and warped floors and ceilings. One of the great things about shooting in New York is that these places still exist. We found a great old Catholic school, over a hundred years old, that had not been touched up in decades. We knew this would be a fantastic location to build on. Once we secured the location, Dina and her team went to work turning an old vestibule into a police precinct desk area.

We also needed to create the Muldoon residence, a tenement in Hell's Kitchen, an old-time pool hall, and an apartment for a high-end prostitute. Dina and her team hit each location out of the park— with a level of detail and nuance that was unsurpassed.

Likewise, Cat created a wardrobe that came to life. These guys were working-class men, who covered a wide spectrum of the current style. Michael Rapaport's character, Bullman, needed to look a little less put together than Muldoon. The younger cops, Austin Stowell's O'Bannon and Brian Wiles's Shea, needed to look sharp, and we referenced some of the sixties icons of the era—from Paul Newman to Steve McQueen in their iconic roles. Liz Masucci's character, Christine, like a lot of women of that era, took her look from Jackie O. And Katrina Bowden's Fortune the prostitute needed to suggest the sex appeal of the era, while looking conservative enough at times to potentially be a schoolteacher.

Another way to sell the era was by populating the streets with cars from the fifties and sixties. Paul's friend, Irv Gooch, owned a picture car lot in New Jersey, a space filled to the brim with cars, trucks, buses, and other vehicles from the era. The problem was that it was one of the worst winters in New York, and there were mountains of snow covering these old cars. We visited the lot and went shopping—picking out period buses, delivery trucks, police radio cars, and plenty of old rides. We made sure that all the other picture cars looked beat-up, dented, and completely authentic. We did not want a show where every car on the street was in pristine condition. It was a challenge getting them out of that lot, where they were packed in like sardines, under ice and snow, and then moving and storing them in New York. Then, on shooting days, we needed dozens ready at up to three locations a day. Many of these cars had a hard time starting, but Irv, an expert mechanic, always came through.

A week before shooting, we had one major presentation, a show-and-tell, when I would walk through about 150 images of our locations, cast, wardrobe, and cinematography. We needed to get Steven's approval first, so we conducted a video conference at a facility on 23rd Street. I talked for about an hour and a half straight, my excitement clear about creating this world. Steven loved it. As did Darryl and Justin. They embraced our desire to abandon the traditional needs of standard coverage that you typically see on TV shows and embrace a more cinematic style, where the camera was always moving. Steven also loved the look we were going for, and expressed his own desire to see this world through a gritty, unpolished lens.

We had only two or three tweaks to make before we pitched Michael Wright and his team at TNT the following day. Like the Spielberg presentation, this one could not have gone better. When it was over, Michael said, "I got nothing. No notes." He pointed to his hard copy of the presentation. "Just do this!"

We were on our way.

SHOOTING

We had made many movies during a New York winter, and the weather always cooperated with us. Given how smoothly everything was running, we hoped the weather gods would smile on this production.

No such luck. New York was bombarded by snowstorm after snowstorm, and bitter cold conditions throughout February and March. This was not the ideal time to be making a period show in New York when nearly all of our scenes took place outside. However, we are a team that has made multiple micro- and low-budget movies. Given our indie background, we had a skill set that would serve us well on this shoot. We knew how to think on our feet, pivot in another direction when trouble came our way, and quickly reshuffle a schedule so we wouldn't lose an hour of precious shooting time. Due to the weather, we were constantly scrambling. But we knew how to find creative solutions when faced with production challenges, and we had far more resources on this show than in past projects. And the greatest resource we had: a seasoned New York crew.

One thing that warmed us up was Steven's regular, comprehensive enthusiasm for the project. He was always the first one to see the dailies, and he would send me a report card on a regular basis. Fortunately, he always loved what he saw, and that gave me and my team more confidence that we were onto something special.

It also helped that our actors, every one of them, were up for

Shooting the final scene of the *Public Morals* pilot

anything. While it's critical to find the right actor for a part, nothing slows down a production more than an actor who is difficult or, even worse, abusive to the crew and other cast mates. Put simply, we have a "no asshole policy" and that applies across the board to anyone on set. We make it a point to do our due diligence on the actors and make sure they cross the talent threshold but are also team players.

Tim Hutton, in particular, set the tone of professionalism. On a bitter cold night, when he had to perform a stunt outside a gin mill, he took fall after fall on the cold, hard concrete, committing every time, always rejecting the option for a stunt double to do the dirty work.

On the coldest day of our shoot, we found ourselves under the Brooklyn Bridge, where Tim, hair wet, was lying in the sand. As the wind howled above him, the frigid water from the East River lapped two feet from his body. And while it was freezing that day, it was one of the best shooting days I've ever had. We used a technocrane to capture the scene in one continuous take: We tracked my character, with the Manhattan Bridge framed behind us, walking up to Hutton, and then had the camera pull up thirty feet in the air. This was the shot to end the pilot episode, and it was a hell of a closing image.

GUESS WHO'S COMING TO SET

Steven Spielberg, as he had suggested earlier, was planning to make a set visit. I hadn't been on a set with him since *Saving Private Ryan*, and that, as we know, was a different circumstance.

I can't say I was calm and collected, but the crew was buzzing with excitement. All of a sudden, they felt a different kind of recognition. Steven is a legend but, at that point, had been only someone on the other end of my e-mail and phone. My team and I grew up heavily influenced by Steven and his movies. We made it a point to introduce Steven to the crew, and meeting him in person and seeing his connection to the material we were all working so hard to capture was a career highlight for us.

As always, Steven was complimentary and supportive and genuinely proud of the project, not as an admirer but as a producer. This was his project as well. We put his director's chair in front of the monitor, and he locked in to the scene. After every take, we would review the playback together. When we executed the shot perfectly, Steven gave the thumbs-up.

To make things even better, my dad was on set that day. He had been with us for about a week, and had worked the months before as my script consultant. My dad and Steven hadn't seen each other since *Saving Private Ryan*, where he and my uncle first regaled Steven with stories of their days on the job. It was a treat to reunite.

It was another one of those special days in the business when you have to step back and take a moment to recognize how lucky you are to be doing the thing you love. I pulled my old man aside and told him this was a moment we needed to savor. He agreed. My dad had supported me from day one and he knew how much hard work had gone into getting here.

We wrapped later that week in an alley in Greenpoint, Brooklyn. The weather had finally warmed up and our spirits were high. After a few speeches from me and various crew members, we retired to the bar where we partied until five in the morning.

Steven Spielberg visiting the *Public Morals* set

EDITING

Unlike movies, the editing process in television is very fast. After we wrapped shooting, we had about two weeks to deliver the film to Steven and then to TNT.

In the same way we hired familiar faces in production, we hired my longtime, trusted editor, Janet Gaynor, and my composer, P. T. Walkley. This show was a dream job for P.T., who is also a singer-songwriter and whose music has long been inspired by the sixties rock we wanted to use in the soundtrack. We also brought on Zak Tucker from Harbor Pictures to supervise the picture and color of the show, as well as Gregg Swiatlowski to supervise sound at Goldcrest Post, a facility we had been using for ten years. Both Zak and Gregg are veterans of our team, each having come aboard on *Nice Guy Johnny*. They had done enormous favors for us on the last three films and now we could repay them.

We felt very lucky to work with TNT—they supported every hire, every crew member, and every vendor I wanted, even though some of our team had not worked consistently in television. I wanted to prove TNT's instincts correct: Support my vision and my team, and we'll produce a kick-ass show on budget and on schedule. Which we did.

After the glowing response from the dailies and the open acknowledgment of how professional, responsible, and talented our team was, it was now time to show the baby. Of course, Steven and his team would get the first look, and we sent it to them on a Friday night. As expected, by Saturday morning, Steven had already seen the pilot twice. His e-mail to me was frame-worthy, saying that we had created a truly great hour of programming, something that needs to be on television. He would vouch for it to the powers that be at

TNT. Darryl and Justin also communicated similar enthusiasm, and we were on our way.

The next week, we delivered to Michael Wright and TNT. As on the Saturday prior, I woke up to a text from Michael that said simply "freaking fantastic." Michael and Steven then began their dialogue about how much they loved the show. Michael had some thoughtful notes, and we continued to shape and hone the cut in preparation for the test screening. Now I just had to get the approval from forty-eight strangers.

TESTING

It was around two P.M., a full hour before we were due at ASI Entertainment, a research facility entrusted with testing our pilot. As always, Aaron made sure we were not late, and we had some time to kill in the brutal valley sun as we cruised up and down Laurel Canyon Boulevard. I told Aaron, "So, here we are again. Another critical day in our careers." He responded, "Yeah, there's no denying that the stakes are high today."

We pulled over on a residential street and discussed a recent article in *The New Yorker* about Norman Lear and the iconic character Archie Bunker. The author Emily Nussbaum suggests that Archie Bunker was the pioneer of the flawed protagonist that now populates the cable landscape. Audiences, to the surprise of some, turned out to like characters with human shortcomings. They related to them. When we thought about Tony Soprano, Don Draper, and Walter White, some of the most iconic characters on television in the last twenty years, it was easy to see that the creators did not pull punches when crafting these leading men. We thought those instincts boded well for *Public Morals.*

It was now time to make our move to the test. After parking, we wound our way through a maze of hallways, featuring posters of what seemed like every hit television show. We settled into a comfortable room with a one-way glass window that overlooked a small theater. We could see the audience, but they could not see us. The research team explained to us that these recruited forty-eight audience members, half men and half women, had a knob that they could turn right or left, depending on how engaged they were in the program. They also had a button to press if they felt the impulse to change the channel.

Then the TNT executives entered, led by Michael Wright. Michael and I have bonded countless times over our shared Irish heritage, and this show has been a source of personal interest for him. He explained, "Look, my love for this show is unwavering. We hate doing these tests, but it will help us if we can clear the norms. If it doesn't, I'll still push like hell for this show."

Michael, as always, put a good spin on it. I had no doubt Steven would also fight to get the show picked up, but we couldn't help but realize that the numbers do matter. While our inner circle had told us how much they loved the pilot, it was no less terrifying to have forty-eight strangers grade the show. For the first time in a while, we were not in control. All we could do was watch the little red and blue lines move up and down our screen as we gauged the audience response.

From the moment the first sequence started, the lines jumped well into the positive territory, and the audience was clearly engaged. While the indicators were positive, we still had to wait for the final scores, the numbers that would be passed along to Atlanta and New York.

Once the screening ended, ASI broke the audience off into two focus groups, men and women. These little rooms also had the one-way windows where we could listen to their guided feedback. After watching these groups talk with interest and excitement about the show, our confidence grew.

Then Michael came over, clutching the results. "Congratulations, Eddie," he said. "This is a great test. You just made my job a lot easier!"

Pretty soon, a couple of six-packs materialized and the creative team celebrated a great moment. Now the wind was solidly at our backs as we sailed toward the May 6 presentation to the head Turner brass. We clinked glasses and, some time later, parted ways on the roof of the scorching-hot parking lot. Aaron and I made our way back over Laurel Canyon and into West Hollywood, a good ten degrees cooler, a perfect 73 degrees. This was another moment to be savored.

A GOOD OMEN

We met Darryl and Justin that night at Dan Tana's, one of my favorite LA spots, probably because it feels like a New York joint and they have one of the best New York strips you'll ever eat. Over the years, we've had countless meals there, often commemorating a high moment in the business, but we could not remember being here under such positive circumstances.

Darryl's family owns a winery in Napa, and he brought their top Cabernet to celebrate. We laughed about the testing process, discussed the show, and looked forward to the beginning of the journey. When Steven first read the script, he described it to Michael as a project that combined elements of *The Wire* and *Serpico*. *Serpico*, if you remember, is the Sidney Lumet film that showcases the Public Morals Division in late sixties and early seventies New York. It stars a young Al Pacino, who plays Frank Serpico, the famous whistleblower who blew the lid on organized police corruption.

As we drank more wine and dug into our steaks, a man at the next table reached his hand over to me. "Hey, Ed," he said with a gravelly voice. Looking over, I clearly recognized the face and the voice: It was Al Pacino, the most famous Public Morals cop in film and television. I had met Al over the years, but was surprised he remembered me. I shook his hand, smiling at the irony. We decided that this was a good omen.

TWENTY-THREE
INDEPENDENT ED

P rior to creating my first television show, *Public Morals*, I made eleven movies in twenty years, and half were considered failures. They either didn't find their audience or they got terrible reviews, and in some cases both. It happened and there are any number of reasons why. In some cases, the film wasn't as good as we thought or the marketing wasn't right. In other cases, we were just unlucky. In hindsight, I can see now that none of that matters. It's not about the box office or the accolades or the money or any of the other perks; it's about the process. The only thing that matters is the process.

If I leave you with anything, it's this: You must love what you do and do it with everything you've got. Stay true to yourself and your work and be prepared for the peaks and valleys that come with a career in Hollywood. There will be periods of time when that thing you do falls out of favor. The key is not to think that you gotta change your game. What you do will come back into favor. As a friend of mine in the music biz recently told me, "Like an old jazz artist, you own your tone. And they can't take that away from you. If not for you, would we have seen this slice of life or gotten this point of view?"

Filmmaker Robert Bresson said it best: "Make visible what, without you, might perhaps never be seen." That's what I've been going for since day one and that's why, after all these ups and downs and highs and lows, I'm still at it.

ACKNOWLEDGMENTS

I would like to thank my parents for a lifetime of support, inspiration, and, over the years, access to their home so I could make my low-budget movies. Thanks to my producing partner, Aaron Lubin, who has been working with me for more than fifteen years and has a far better memory than I do about most of the details from these movies. Gratitude to my good friend Todd Gold, who collaborated with me on the writing of the book and teased out some great anecdotes from our lengthy conversations. Thanks to Jacqui Rivera, my former assistant, who was a great sounding board during the final phase of writing, as well as Sinead Daly for her input as well. And finally, a big thank-you to my wife for giving me the idea to write this book in the first place.

ABOUT THE AUTHOR

Lauded by critics and audiences alike, Ed Burns gained international recognition for his first feature film, *The Brothers McMullen*, which premiered in competition at the 1995 Sundance Film Festival, winning the Grand Jury Prize. The film, which Burns wrote, directed, and starred in, was shot on a budget of only $25,000 and went on to gross more than $10 million at the domestic box office, making it the most profitable film of 1995. The film also won Best First Feature at the 1996 Independent Spirit Awards.

Burns's second film, the romantic comedy *She's the One* starring Jennifer Aniston and Cameron Diaz, reinforced Burns's versatile talent as a writer, director, and actor able to simultaneously and successfully wear multiple hats.

His eleventh feature film as a writer, director, and actor is the drama *The Fitzgerald Family Christmas*, which had its world premiere at the 2012 Toronto International Film Festival and stars Kerry Bishé, Connie Britton, Caitlin FitzGerald, Ed Lauter, and Michael McGlone.

Burns continues to write, direct, star in, and produce his films, including the Paramount Classics relationship comedy *Sidewalks of New York*, *Purple Violets*, *Nice Guy Johnny*, and *Newlyweds*. In a groundbreaking deal, *Purple Violets* was the first feature film to premiere exclusively on iTunes. Burns expanded on this new model of digital distribution to include cable Video on Demand to reach even wider audiences and successfully released two films, *Nice Guy Johnny* and *Newlyweds*, via these platforms in 2010 and 2011.

As an actor, Burns starred opposite Tom Hanks and Matt Damon in Steven Spielberg's critically acclaimed World War II epic *Saving Private Ryan*. He also starred in the thriller *15 Minutes* opposite Robert De Niro, *Confidence* opposite Dustin Hoffman, and the Twentieth Century Fox romantic comedy hit *27 Dresses* opposite Katherine Heigl.

Burns most recently starred in three-time Academy Award–nominated filmmaker Frank Darabont's event series *Mob City* as legendary gangster Bugsy Siegel for TNT, and he is currently shooting his series *Public Morals*, which he created, stars in, and executive produces alongside Steven Spielberg and Amblin Television for TNT.

Ed Burns was born in Woodside, Queens, and raised on Long Island. While at Hunter College in New York City, Burns switched his focus from English to filmmaking before quickly moving on to make *The Brothers McMullen*.

He lives in New York City with his wife and two children.